THE EVOLUTION OF
COLONIAL ARCHITECTURE

Other volumes in the
ARCHITECTURAL TREASURES
OF EARLY AMERICA
Series

THE EVOLUTION OF COLONIAL ARCHITECTURE

Vol. IX in the Architectural Treasures of Early America Series

From material originally published as
The White Pine Series of Architectural Monographs
edited by
Russell F. Whitehead and Frank Chouteau Brown

Lisa C. Mullins, Editor

Preface by Roy Underhill,
Master Housewright at Colonial Williamsburg

A Publication of The National Historical Society

DISTRIBUTED BY

THE MAIN STREET PRESS • Pittstown, New Jersey

Published by
The National Historical Society
2245 Kohn Road, Box 8200
Harrisburg, Pennsylvania 17105

Distributed by
The Main Street Press
William Case House
Pittstown, New Jersey 08867

Distributed simultaneously in Canada by
McGraw-Hill Ryerson Ltd.
330 Progress Avenue
Scarborough, Ontario M1P 2Z5

Printed in the United States of America

10 9 8 7 6 5 4 3 2 1

Library of Congress Cataloging-in-Publication Data

The Evolution of colonial architecture.
    (Architectural treasures of early America; 9)
    1. Architecture, Domestic—New England. 2. Architec-
ture, Colonial—New England. 3. Decoration and
ornament, Architectural—New England. 4. Building, Brick—New
England. I. Mullins, Lisa C. II. Underhill,
Roy.   III. National Historical Society. IV. Series:
Architectural treasures of Early America (Harrisburg,
Pa.); 9
NA7210.E96   1988   720'.974   87-14206
ISBN 0-918678-28-5
ISBN 1-55562-049-3 (Main Street)

The original photographs reproduced in this publication are from
the collection of drawings and photographs in "The White Pine
Monograph Series, Collected and Edited by Russell F. Whitehead,
The George P. Lindsay Collection." The collection, part of
the research and reference collections of The American Institute
of Architects, Washington, D.C., was acquired by the Institute
in 1955 from the Whitehead estate, through the cooperation of Mrs.
Russell F. Whitehead, and the generosity of the Weyerhauser Timber
Company, which purchased the collection for presentation to the
Institute. The research and reference collections of the Institute are
available for public use. A written request for such use is required so
that space may be reserved and assistance made available.

CONTENTS

LIVING IN THE PAST

The surviving houses of early America are the "Rosetta Stones" of the American past. So writes Joseph Everett Chandler in Chapter 1 of this volume. But even after an early house is restored, endless questions remain. When was the house built? What were the rooms called? Who used them? What was in them? Just as the decipherment of the Rosetta Stone opened a window on ancient Egypt, new techniques in the study of early America have begun to answer these questions about life in the early American home.

The problem of determining precisely when a house was built has been largely met by dendrochronology—the science of dating timbers by matching variations in the width of the growth rings in the wood. A tree will grow better in a wet year than in a dry year, and this variation will be recorded in the width of the rings. First developed in Arizona in 1929, "endless tree" patterns made from timbers of overlapping generations have now been constructed for many areas of the east coast. By taking a sample from a house timber and matching the patterns, you can tell in what year, and even in what season of the year, the trees were felled. Of course, many houses were built with timbers reused from earlier buildings, which has led to some spectacular errors in dating by this method.

Another dating technique is based on the invariable by-product of human occupation—garbage. In the garbage are clues about the people who produced it. (Even the way the garbage is thrown out reflects cultural patterns. Some cultures tend to throw their garbage out the back door, others tend to throw it out the front door.) Some of the most helpful artifacts for dating a site are the broken stems of clay tobacco pipes. Fragile, and thus constantly discarded in great numbers, they show a steady decrease in the diameter of their bore over the years. In 1620 the average bore diameter was one eighth of an inch. Decreasing by 1/64 of an inch every thirty years, the diameter was one sixteenth of an inch by 1800. Should you find a pipe stem while digging in your garden, and you have a set of drill bits handy, see which bit fits into the bore of the pipestem. Just be sure that you are not dealing with fill dirt that was brought in from another site!

Ceramic cups and plates are also easily broken, but again, like pipe stems, the discarded fragments are indestructible. Changes in the types and styles of ceramics can date a site to within a decade or so. As with all the methods of the architectural detective, ceramics hold their share of red herrings. Poorer people tend to have more out-of-date ceramics, acquired only second hand. Simply put, the garbage of poor people looks older than that of the rich.

The patterns of the poor can be hard to discover, and the traces of the poorest can be all but invisible. Until recently, no one could explain the clusters of storage pits found near some houses. Because there was no evidence of foundations around them, they did not fit any known pattern. At a few sites, however, archaeologists did find the outlines of very insubstantial structures around such pits. These pits are now considered indicative of slave housing that was so lightly built that no foundations survived.

Ironically, the occasion of the death of our ancestors has provided the best tool for bringing their homes to life. Even before the turn of this century, historians were studying early estate inventories to understand the world of the people who lived in these houses. When a man died, the appraisers of the estate would enter a room, record the items in the room and their value, and then move on to the next room. Where both the building and the inventory have survived, (as in the case of the 1668 inventory of the Fairbanks House,) quantitative studies can give us a new look at the use of the house. We can evaluate the relative importance of the rooms by determining the value of the contents per square foot of floor space. We can learn how much floor space was taken up by the objects in the room, and how much was left to the inhabitants. Images of living spaces that vanished centuries ago are being recreated every day; on paper, on computer screens, and in new brick and timber.

Some people, however, are not content to just look at the past through a window. Some want to throw open the diamond-paned casement and crawl inside. This is the most glamorous type of historical research — the "Kon-Tiki," experimental archaeology approach. Long applied to prehistoric activities, many museums and individuals are trying living experiments; replicating processes and structures to learn how patterns may have evolved, hoping to discover previously unseen connections. To find out how much firewood a Pilgrim household would need for a winter, one "simply" lives like a Pilgrim in a Pilgrim house for a winter or two. As subjective and uncontrolled as these experiments may seem, it may be the only way of testing conclusions. The day may come when the accusation of "living in the past," will be the highest compliment a student of early American architecture can receive.

ROY UNDERHILL
MASTER HOUSEWRIGHT
COLONIAL WILLIAMSBURG

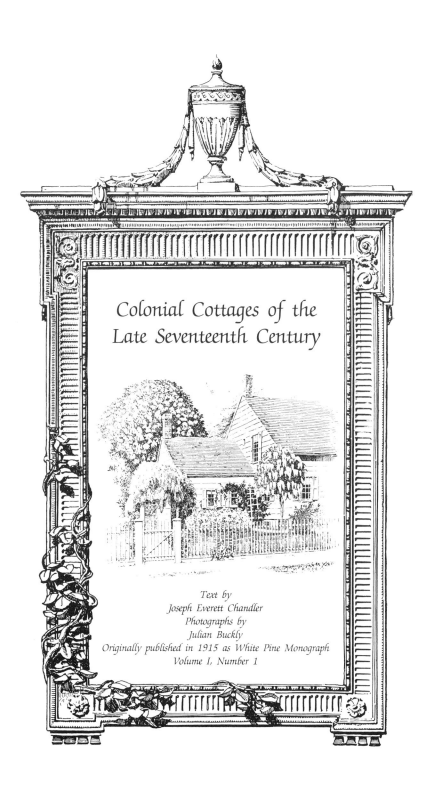

Colonial Cottages of the Late Seventeenth Century

Text by
Joseph Everett Chandler
Photographs by
Julian Buckly
Originally published in 1915 as White Pine Monograph
Volume I, Number 1

Photograph by Julian Buckly

Detail of Gable
CAPEN HOUSE, TOPSFIELD, MASSACHUSETTS
Built during the second half of the seventeenth century; an example of the framed overhang
type. The central bracket supporting the gable overhang is the original; the drops are restored.

COLONIAL COTTAGES OF MASSACHUSETTS
DURING THE LATTER HALF
OF THE SEVENTEENTH CENTURY

WE read with absorbing interest how students of Egyptian archaeology found in the Rosetta Stone, with the aid of other inscriptions, the key to the hieroglyphics on the tombs and the obelisks, and by it were enabled to interpret to the modern world the records of bygone centuries. Wonderfully picturesque and instructive to us have been the translations of these Egyptian records, revealing as they do the daily life of those days. Seldom do we stop to think that a large part of the history of the days of our own forefathers lies recorded in the very walls of the houses they built. The records are preserved in a somewhat different way, it is true, but without the few houses that remain, we should be at a loss to know in what manner of domicile the early colonists lived their lives, since the rare written documents of that period make slight mention of the houses. Were these buildings not preserved, we might be picturing the colonists of New England as living for many years in rough log huts, whereas actually such rude shelters were rapidly replaced by houses of more or less finished craftsmanship, and there are indications that even during the first fifty years subsequent to the settlement by the Pilgrims in 1620, considerable thought was expended upon the aesthetic as well as upon the practical side of the problem.

Some of the early craftsmen who became our carpenter-builders in New England brought with them from the mother country certain traditional methods of construction, and for a period followed the ways with which they were familiar. But the new country, with its rigorous climate, rapid temperature changes and frequent searching storms, as well as the completely new materials with which they were obliged to work, soon caused them to adapt their work to the new conditions, with results which were utterly distinct from any work of the mother country.

Unfortunately many of these early domiciles have been destroyed, some because the small villages of which they once formed a part have now grown into cities, while others have been torn down and replaced with newer and more pretentious structures because of the persistent (and perhaps regrettable) love of change characteristic of the American people. Nevertheless, in the eddies and quiet harbors of the territory inhabited by the early colonists there can still be found a few examples of the dwellings of our forefathers, which seem to express in their sturdy frames something of that strength of character which the definite purpose, the aspirations and the hopes of their original occupants quickly gathered from the new soil. Their point of view of life was peculiarly bound up in, and expressed by, their family shells—their homes.

There was not much masonry used in our early domestic architecture. The foundations were of stone, frequently laid up in clay dug from the cellars; the spaces between the timbers of the framework were filled with soft brick of home manufacture, often laid up in clay mortar; the chimneys were of stone or of brick, sometimes of the two in combination, with the hearths of the fireplaces of smooth, large stones, or of hard brick, or of large, heavy tiles brought from the mother country.

These few portions of the house were the only ones not built of wood, for the framework, the floors and the walls alike bear testimony to the ease with which the native woods were employed to further comfort and beauty. Undoubtedly their builders gave thought to the beautiful, even in those stern days of wresting a livelihood from the new and difficult soil and the waters which isolated them from the rest of the world. Why otherwise should the summer beams which carried the overhanging second stories have their edges chamfered, with beautiful mouldings carved into the chamfer, and stopped at the ends with the familiar "lamb's tongue" ornament? The amount of care lavished on these early buildings is surprising. At the same time, had the material been oak, as it was in the English houses, it could never have been executed with the small means at the disposal of the colonists. Instead of oak the colonists used the strong, easily worked, comparatively light and entirely durable white pine, the best of the plentiful native woods. The mass of the house as well as the details was studied by their craftsmen-builders; witness the many cases where they were built with overhanging second stories on the front or sides and occasionally having the gable ends treated in a similar way. This overhang was probably reminiscent of the

Detail of Pendant
OLD BROWN HOUSE, HAMILTON, MASSACHUSETTS

The overhang is unusual in being a framed end showing endgirt
moulded and chamfered. This is a fine type of drop ornament depending from the posts framed into the projecting second end-girt. The
House of the Seven Gables in Salem was found to be similar to this house.

random widths, inclining to be very broad, the
edges matched and the juncture carrying a series
of mouldings which were flush with the faces
of the boards. In some cases a type of decoration has been found of a curious dentil cut into
these mouldings, which are then run between
the chimney girt and posts, on the edge of the
boarding. The under flooring of the upper
rooms was exposed and thereby formed a
roughly paneled ceiling between the girders
and joists, and this flooring was as interesting
seen from above as from below, for it was made
of great slabs of white pine held in place with
wooden pegs. In spite of the fact that they
were often two feet in width, because of the
nature of the material they show little shrink-
age and few cracks.

The posts, girts, summer beams and joists
were usually exposed in the interior, and were
frequently of such great size that the construction might almost be called massive, although
they were put together in the most character-
ful way, tongued and pinned and oftentimes
decorated with mouldings and chamfers. This
construction, so direct and convincing, has a
feeling quite distinct from that later work which
usually comes to mind when the word "Colonial"
is used, it being rather Gothic than Classic in its
charm and spirit.

The inside walls were usually plastered even

traditional English construction, but was un-
questionably carried out because it was picturesque, and not because of its utility or ease
of construction. Very frequently the overhang
was embellished with brackets, drops and
chamfered beams or girts, which show considerable care and a decided feeling for form in
their selection.

The overhang on the front, which was a more
usual position for it than on the ends of the
building, generally had four carved ornamental
drops depending from the four girts, two at the
ends and two on the extension of the central
chimney girts, when the projection of the second
story was of "framed" construction and sufficient to receive them. Possibly, at times,
brackets were used at either side of the front
door, and certainly when gable ends projected
they were frequently carried on brackets, sometimes of ornamental form, as was the case in
the Capen House, in Topsfield, Massachusetts,
which is in many ways one of the most interesting of the remaining examples.

The interiors likewise were not built as was
most convenient, but show that care and
thought were displayed in treating the novel
conditions encountered by the early builders so
as to produce an interesting and often beautiful
effect. For example, many of the houses had
their interiors ceiled vertically with boards of

Detail of Corner Post
OLD BRAY HOUSE, WEST GLOUCESTER, MASSACHUSETTS

The corner post — "shouldered" — is roughly carved. It
is a piece of ornamented construction of great interest.

in the houses where the chimney end partitions were covered with wood; and as most of the early work was unpainted and left to darken with age, the flooring only being sanded or scrubbed, the combination of color was indescribably warm, rich and satisfying, and completed most satisfactorily rooms of excellent structural design. The days have happily not gone by when many people consider this kind of an interior much more attractive than one in which the walls are covered with elaborate work and painted innumerable coats, rubbed down and glossed to a "piano finish." There is at least one recent instance where an owner has built his home in the form of this early period, leaving the marks of the adze and other implements on the wood, following the old methods of construction carefully, the result being a modern house thoroughly American in spirit and of old-time honesty and charm of feeling.

These houses were in many ways different from the later and better known Colonial type on the exterior as well as within; the roofs were steeper, the houses thinner, and what little detail there was, was of forms founded on domestic Gothic work rather than on those of the period of the Classic Revival; the chimneys usually were long and comparatively thin, instead of massive and square as we should have expected, and were frequently embellished by projecting pilasters. An example of this sort of chimney may be seen in the Boardman House at Saugus, as well as in the Corbett House at Ipswich.

The green and white of the conventional Colonial was likewise a thing of later development, for many of the old houses have never had a coat of paint. Others were probably not painted until many years after their construction, and the fact that so many of the older buildings have remained in good condition until this day, without any paint at all, is extraordinary testimony to the durability of the materials used in their construction.

These houses, built in the stress of strenuous early times, do not furnish us much for study or emulation in the way of detail, except that most admirable kind which was applied to the important constructional pieces of framing. These forms are so different from those we usually employ and are of such honesty and charm that they deserve to be far more extensively known than is the case at present. Therefore it seems quite appropriate that this series of architectural monographs should commence with the depiction of these early efforts of house-building in one of the foremost and most individual of the original states, and from which early domestic architecture gradually evolved that type which is commonly referred to today as the Colonial Style.

OLD BRAY HOUSE, WEST GLOUCESTER, MASSACHUSETTS

An example of the hewn overhang type of construction. The large size of
the cornice would suggest that a plaster cove cornice had once been used here.

CAPEN HOUSE, TOPSFIELD, MASSACHUSETTS

An example of the framed overhang type built during the second half of the seventeenth century. The drops were restored after the Brown House at Hamilton, Massachusetts. The bracket in the center of the gable overhang is the original one; those at the sides of the doorway are reproduced from this, and are a sensible embellishment, but not as constructional as the girt-supported posts and the drops usual in this position. The use of drop ornaments in the gable is questionable. The fenestration has been unchanged in restoration, although leaded sash have been substituted in place of "double-hung" sash.

OLD LOW HOUSE, WENHAM, MASSACHUSETTS

The original house was built in the second half of the seventeenth century, with framed overhang, front and side. In the eighteenth century the addition in front of this was added, the chimneys both being of this latter period. The house is a picturesque growth and combination of the two periods.

CORBETT HOUSE, IPSWICH, MASSACHUSETTS

Of the hewn overhang type and built during the second half of the seventeenth century. The gable end overhang is slight but continuous, with moulded edges of framing where showing extensively. The chimney is an excellent example of the "pilastered" type belonging to this period. The fenestration is probably original as to location and size, but it is thought double-hung sash have been substituted for the single leaded sash.

OLD ELLERY HOUSE, GLOUCESTER, MASSACHUSETTS

Of the framed overhang type. Built during the second half of the seventeenth century. The roof has projecting gable ends with lean-to. The chimney is larger and nearer square than is usual in this kind of house. The original drops from the ends of the second-story posts have been removed and small ball-shaped ornaments substituted.

Photograph by Julian Buckl...

SALTONSTALL-WHIPPLE HOUSE—BETWEEN 1636-1675—IPSWICH, MASSACHUSETTS

Hewn end overhang type. The overhang is here entirely at the end of the house, and in both the second story and attic. The chimney is a good example of this period, with projection at back, indicating early additions to it when the lean-to was added. The windows have been restored according to legend with triple sash, but the panes of glass should not be divided by wood muntins, but rather with lead. The house is one of the claimants against the Fairbanks House for the distinction of being the oldest house now standing in America. It was undoubtedly, however, built at a later date.

The Seventeenth Century Connecticut House

Text by
Harold Donaldson Eberlein
Originally published in 1919 as White Pine Monograph
Volume V, Number 1

Detail of Entrance
GOLDSMITH HOUSE — c1700 — BETWEEN GUILFORD AND BRANFORD, CONNECTICUT

THE SEVENTEENTH CENTURY CONNECTICUT HOUSE

WITH apologies to the author of the famous schoolboy Hibernianism, committed in translating into English the opening sentence of Caesar, *De Bello Gallico*, we may say that all of early Connecticut was "quartered into three halves." Of these, the first and most anciently settled was the region round about Hartford, including the towns of Windsor and Wethersfield and the tracts bordering thereon. This was in 1636. Not long afterwards—to be historically exact, in 1638—came the New Haven group of settlements, while in 1646 followed the laying out of New London, to which latter sphere of colonizing influence belonged the town of Norwich. There was, it is true, a fourth early plantation (1637) at Saybrook, and on the lands immediately adjacent thereto at the mouth of the Connecticut River; but as this colonizing venture never attained the political nor numerical growth of the "three halves" previously mentioned, and was more or less identified with the Hartford group, we may pass it without further mention here, interesting though it be historically and architecturally, since the houses of the Connecticut River Valley have already been discussed in a previous chapter.

Our present concern is with seventeenth century Connecticut houses other than those in the valley settlements, or what is known as the Connecticut Colony, embracing the river towns and their offshoots. That means to say that most of our material is drawn from the New Haven settlement, for, thanks to the gentle incendiary attentions of Benedict Arnold, the burning of New London left but little of the seventeenth century work undestroyed in that city. The other seventeenth century structures in the neighboring country are virtually analogous to the New Haven types or else obviously affected by Rhode Island characteristics. Lest the reader be led to expect too great a diversity between the different local types, it is well to preface our detailed examination by observing that, although the "joints visible in the [early] political structure of Connecticut were faithfully repeated in the architecture of the first century of the colony's existence," the differences are not sharp and are chiefly to be noted in matters of detail in such particulars as resulted from "the constructive preferences of the carpenters and masons who literally founded and built the commonwealth, and who, through their successive apprentices, handed down their different craft traditions." The differences are, however, quite sufficient to make study and comparison both interesting and profitable.

The New Haven sphere of influence embraced the towns to the east and west, and the small settlements for a short distance inland from them—Guilford, Branford, Milford, Stratford, Fairfield and their immediate hinterland. Colonists settled in all of these places within a year or two of the colony's planting. And the men of the New Haven Colony were, all things considered, of more substantial estate than any other body of planters who sat down within the boundaries of the present state of Connecticut. They were such men as Governor Theophilus Eaton, Thomas Gregson, the Reverend John Davenport and Isaac Allerton, all of whom had houses befitting their substance and civic importance, while other men of easy means, as affluence was then reckoned, also erected dwellings by no means contemptible. There is also a sufficient number of the houses built in the immediately succeeding period to give us a very accurate idea of the average seventeenth century Connecticut dwelling. In discussing them we may, for the sake of convenience, follow Mr. Isham's classification of two closely related types of seventeenth century house—the one built prior to 1670 or 1675, and the other built between these dates and the end of the century. One of the chief items of differentiation between the two was the treatment of the lean-to. In the former type it was generally an independent and somewhat later addition; in

pal mass and the lean-to[2] (as frequently in the earlier type where the lean-to was a subsequent addition), with a slightly gentler slope thence downward; a buxom stone or brick chimney stack rising from the center of the roof line, the top of the stack capped "with one or more thin courses, which project like moulded bands," and sometimes also another projection or necking below and distinct from the capping; last of all, the overhang, one of the most interesting features for purely architectural reasons and one that

PHILO BISHOP HOUSE—c1665—GUILFORD, CONNECTICUT

the latter it was commonly incorporated in the original plan and erected as an integral portion of the body of the structure.

Both types were approximately the same in the contour of their mass—an oblong rectangular main body containing two floors, with an attic in the steep pitched roof which sloped down in the rear almost to the ground, covering the lean-to, and displayed either one unbroken pitch[1] (as usually in the later type) or else a break at the line of junction between the princi-

vastly contributed likewise to the strongly individual expression of the contour. In the middle of the front was the house door with two windows at each side, while a row of five windows generally filled the front of the second floor, or else there was one window on each side of the door and three on the second floor. From an inspection of the exterior it is possible to form a correct idea of the interior plan. On the ground floor were two rooms, the "hall" or living room, which in the earliest times served for kitchen

[1]*Vide* Acadian House, Guilford, page 26

[2]*Vide* Baldwin House, Branford; Walker House, Stratford; and Bishop House, Guilford, pages 27, 30 and 22.

also, and the parlor. In the middle of the house, between the rooms, was the great stone chimney structure with a capacious fireplace in each room. The house door opened into a shallow entry or "porch." There, opposite the door and backed up against the masonry of the chimney, a stair of three broken flights ascended to the second floor, where there were two chambers, with their fireplaces, corresponding to the plan of the ground floor. A stair back of the chimney led from one chamber into the attic. Where the

houses shows that the foregoing simple plan was closely adhered to almost without exception; and when there were any variations, they were trifling.

The framing was sometimes of hard pine, sometimes of oak, and occasionally both were used. It is worthy of note that the framing is still in admirable condition except where it has been subjected to the grossest neglect and exposed to insidious leaks. The exterior casing of clapboards was of white pine, not infrequently

STARR HOUSE — c1665 — GUILFORD, CONNECTICUT

lean-to was a subsequent addition, it contained a kitchen and sometimes a small bedchamber. A fireplace was added and a flue built up along the back of the original chimney, whose form, above the roof, now became T-shaped instead of rectangular. Above the ground floor of the lean-to there might or might not be a chamber. Where the lean-to, as in the house of the second type, formed a part of the original scheme, its ground plan was the same, but provision was made for second floor chambers, usually on a level with the "hall" and parlor chambers. Examination of the remaining seventeenth century

left to the coloring agencies of the weather. Man, far more than time or weather, is to blame for the disconcertingly altered conditions that often confront the visitor who endeavors to visualize the pristine appearance of these old houses. The local carpenter of the nineteenth century, who was not an archaeologist nor an antiquary and, unlike his predecessors of the seventeenth and eighteenth centuries, apparently altogether devoid of architectural appreciation, reverence or imagination, was the worst offender. If clapboards were to be renewed, he did not scruple to saw off brackets and moulded drops or even wholly to conceal overhangs and chamfered girts if it suited his whim and convenience. Nor did he hesitate otherwise to obliterate sundry architectural refinements that constituted no small degree of the ancient and rightful charm of the seventeenth century dwelling. That so much of the original aspect of the houses illustrated still remains is a matter for real gratulation. Successive occupants, through an ill-considered obsession to follow the latest fashion, have also been much to blame for senseless and

enteenth or early eighteenth century when the fashion of low transoms with small rectangular lights (*vide* the door of the Bishop House in Guilford and others) was becoming popular. It is more than likely that new doors and doorways were installed, in many cases, in the early years of the eighteenth century at the same time that leaded casements were abandoned and the window apertures altered for the reception of double-hung sashes. As an instance of this may be mentioned the door of the Bishop House in Guilford:

HYLAND-WILDMAN HOUSE, GUILFORD, CONNECTICUT

regrettable changes. At their instance the external features that suffered the most conspicuous change were doors, doorways and windows.

The original doors exhibited interesting and distinctive paneling, and the doorways, though severely simple, were well considered in composition and detail. One of the earliest doors and doorways may be seen in the Baldwin House at Branford. The frame is simple but vigorous. While door and frame may not be coeval with the building of the house, they are very early, and the square lights, cut in the heads of the three upper panels, are obviously a later "improvement," probably dating from the late sev-

the method of paneling, the moulded capping and the transom of the five rectangular lights are all earlier in type than the date of erection. Again, in the Walker House at Stratford, one is tempted to believe that the door itself and the fluted pilasters of the doorway, along with such elements of a scrolled pediment as are still visible beneath the very much later added porch, were applied when the windows were changed. Time and again both doors and doorways were ruthlessly sacrificed in irresponsible fits of modernism. While eighteenth century alterations, both early and late, were often meritorious, and at least decent, the monstrous nineteenth century

HYLAND-WILDMAN HOUSE — 1668 — GUILFORD, CONNECTICUT
Showing detail of hewn overhang, chamfered girt and brackets for post at each side of door.

ACADIAN HOUSE — c1670 — GUILFORD, CONNECTICUT

BALDWIN HOUSE — c1645 — BRANFORD, CONNECTICUT

aberrations of uninspired stock millwork are unpardonable and revolting examples of proprietary vandalism.

All the windows, save those that have escaped the intolerable desecration of recent sashes with large panes, exhibit the double-hung sashes with small panes and wide muntins that supplanted the earlier diamond-paned leaded casements in the fore part of the eighteenth century.

Another significant change that seems to have taken place concurrently with the alteration of the windows was the introduction of a cornice and oftentimes also of moulded barge boards. At first there was no cornice and the only attempt at architectural amenity at the eaves seems to have consisted occasionally of cutting away the under side of the projecting rafter ends so that they were perceptibly larger at the outer extremity than where they left the plate. Sometimes the rafter ends were merely boxed in — if such construction was not original, and it does not appear to have been — as in the Bishop House in Guilford; at other times the rafter ends were sawed off and replaced by a thin moulded board cornice and the moulding was now and again extended to the embellishment of the barge boards. These mouldings showed great restraint and refinement of profile and are unmistakably of the type belonging to the early eighteenth century. Examples of these refined cornice additions may be seen in the Baldwin House at Branford, the Walker House at Stratford, where the moulding is also run around beneath the overhangs and breaks out to form cappings for the window frames, and in the Hyland-Wildman House at Guilford, where, in addition to the several other features, the moulded embellishment occurs on the

Detail of Doorway
BALDWIN HOUSE, BRANFORD, CONNECTICUT

barge boards as well, by way of a special amenity.

Through the towns of the New Haven region considerable variations are to be seen in the use of the overhang. Sometimes it occurs only on the front of the house. Again, it extends around the sides, as in the Hyland-Wildman House. Still again, there is a gable overhang as well as the overhang between the first and second floors, as in the Walker, Tuttle and Goldsmith houses. At times there is only the gable overhang, as in the Bishop House and the Starr houses in Guilford, while some of the houses, like the Baldwin House and the Acadian House, have no overhang at all. We also find one clearly defined form that is distinctively characteristic of the New Haven locality —the *hewn* as distinguished from the *framed* overhang, the latter belonging more particularly to the Hartford region, the Connecticut Colony, and to Massachusetts. An admirable example of the hewn overhang appears in the Hyland-Wildman House in Guilford. In the framing for these hewn overhangs the posts for their whole height are of one stick of timber. The full size — sometimes as much as 15 inches square — occurs in the second floor and from this excess of bulk is hewn out the bracket that seemingly supports the overhang. Below the bracket, the post is dressed down to far slimmer dimensions. With this form of overhang the projection is much less than where there is a framed overhang and there are no turned or moulded drops. The girts were often elaborately chamfered on their lower outer edge and stopped with moulded stops, as may be seen by the illustrations of the Hyland-Wildman House.

From considerations of solicitude for the picturesque in architecture, it is to be regretted domestic architecture should ever be arrived at, for we are a mixed people in our varied racial derivations; but it is not too much to expect—rather, it is altogether feasible and logical—that we should hold to and emphasize our historical background by cultivating the types that have grown with the centuries and proved their fitness by long use. The seventeenth century Connecticut type represents a straight, vital and logical process of evolution from English precedent; it expresses locality and racial derivation, and its perpetuation is eminently reasonable and, as proved by centuries of experience, suited to the climate and manner of life of the people.

Another point that commends the early American types to our close attention at this particular time is their simplicity, combined with dignity and adaptability to domestic requirements reduced to the lowest terms. Postbellum conditions in many places have dictated a far-reaching simplification of domestic *ménage*, and the solution of the problem thus perforce imposed upon us cannot be found in a more appropriate quarter than in the early types that so faithfully reflect the simple but dignified conditions under which our forebears lived.

Detail of Doorway
PHILO BISHOP HOUSE, GUILFORD, CONNECTICUT

that in many later instances the hewn overhang degenerated into mere lines of slight projection across the faces or ends of houses (*vide* Goldsmith House) and that the hewn brackets and chamfered girts wholly disappeared—a change, however, not at all unnatural in view of the very slight projection originally exhibited by the hewn overhang. Even in its sadly emasculated estate, the overhang has a distinct architectural value. It breaks the depressing monotony of a clapboarded wall, gives an agreeable relief of shadow and imparts a degree of charm that should appeal to the severely practical-minded person in the light of an observation made by a highly successful manufacturer and "captain of industry," to wit, that "beauty is the most utilitarian asset we possess." On the same score we may also address a plea to the hard-headed practicality of the case-hardened utilitarian anent the chimneys, which, with their capping and the resultant relief of contour, line and shadow, are well worth perpetuating today.

We frequently hear allusions to the feasibility of developing an American type of domestic architecture. It is too much and unreasonable to expect that any one uniform type of American

Detail of Doorway
WALKER HOUSE, STRATFORD, CONNECTICUT

STARR HOUSE — c1665 — GUILFORD, CONNECTICUT

WALKER HOUSE — c1670 — STRATFORD, CONNECTICUT

HALE HOUSE, SOUTH COVENTRY, CONNECTICUT

HOLLISTER HOUSE — c1675 — SOUTH GLASTONBURY, CONNECTICUT

GOLDSMITH HOUSE — c1700 — BETWEEN GUILFORD AND BRANFORD, CONNECTICUT

Houses of Bennington, Vermont, and Vicinity

Text by
Cameron Clark
Photographs by
Kenneth Clark
Originally published in 1922 as White Pine Monograph
Volume VIII, Number 5

GENERAL DAVID ROBINSON HOUSE, OLD BENNINGTON, VERMONT
A unique adaptation of the Palladian window used frequently in the vicinity of Bennington.

HOUSES OF BENNINGTON, VERMONT, AND VICINITY

WE are continually reading more or less romantic tales of early colonial life woven in and about houses with low-ceilinged rooms whose adze-hewn beams, dark with time and cavernous fireplaces, bring forth memories of a past filled with the simplicity of a cheerful hospitality. These descriptions, while adequate and true as to detail in recalling the past, seldom fail to include the time-worn bromide "They knew how to build in those days." So naturally one might be led to believe that here is the reason for the present revival of interest in Colonial architecture. But if this were true we would see at every hand replicas of this wonderful era, having true beamed ceilings and corner posts with braces projecting into the room. This is not the case, however, and it is not because of plumbing, wiring, or the other practical necessities of a modern house, but for the simple fact that the present day builder asks for the Colonial style because of its exterior beauty rather than for any merits of good old-fashioned construction.

The secret of this desire for the Colonial has been the result of an unconscious appreciation of the color and texture as well as the form of these early houses. The motorist, passing through one of the quiet old villages with its ancient elms shading the beautiful old houses, cannot but retain delightful impressions of their simplicity and charm, and carry away with him a desire to recreate for himself something of that same potent quality which lingers in his mind. The dark roofs with their huge old chimneys, the green shutters, hung against broad white clapboards, shingled or weather-beaten surfaces, as well as the perfect detail of the ornament used on old doorways, cornices, and porches, serve to create an impulse for better building and unconsciously cause a truer appreciation of the relative value of textures, color, and form.

While methods of construction are, today, slightly different, due to the change in conditions and in the variety of inventions, still the results may readily be, to all intents, identical. The material is always the same, though the nearby forest is changed to the nearby lumberyard. The old beams, so readily felled, squared with an adze, and hoisted into place to bear the weight of construction, are substituted today by beams of a uniform size, sawed by mechanical means and of an adequate strength for the load they are to bear. And so on through the details of construction, for what we emphasize as accounting for the charm and permanency of old work can be as readily obtained today should we so desire. We need not necessarily follow the early methods, if the proper relation of values in the Colonial detail is understood and studied in the design. The early builders did their work in the simplest and most practical way possible to them — if we were to employ their methods we should have no better results than by using modern methods, and would only incur an unnecessary amount of labor and expense.

There are such a variety of details to be understood. Take, for example, the clapboards; their width or exposure to the weather is of vital importance, their edges may be rounded by many coats of paint, or possibly they may have little half-round beading at the drip edge. What is their relation to the cornice boards, door and window frames? How do they meet the underside of the cornice and finish at the base? Are they surrounded by a plain or moulded surface?

took on a more studied and classical character, recalling in a thoroughly adequate manner the most perfect Georgian and Adam detail. As the early craftsmen designed they had always the actual structure in mind, a light here and a shadow there, the suitability of the detail they adapted, and they were not fooled as many of our modern designers have been by the sparkle achieved by lines crossed at the ends, inevitable axis lines and facile swerves of the pencil on paper. Modern American architecture has often been cursed because of clever draughtsmen who

HINSDALE HOUSE, NORTH BENNINGTON, VERMONT
Another example of the use of the adapted Palladian window.

What about the width of these clapboards? It is the finesse thus displayed by the early builder that causes us to exclaim as we approach and study his work. It is these things that combine to make his achievement pleasing.

As time went on the early builder developed more studied and elaborate detail; this, added to his already beautiful use of plain surfaces, served to enhance the proportion of his doors, windows, and cornices. The early examples were naturally quaint and rather archaic, with odd curves and shapes, and were only a step removed from the forms of the old world which they were trying to recall and emulate. Documents were gradually assembled and the designs

see only the paper in front of them rather than the structure beyond.

There are other weaknesses that our draughtsmen must overcome before we achieve that atmosphere of repose and respectability associated with the old houses. For instance the proneness to indulge in petty conceits, sprinkling them liberally over the design; working all of their pet motifs into the one before them. They should be more conservative and use possibly two in an effective manner, thereby adding visibly to the result and gaining a design of a more restful and pleasing character. Among the little conceits referred to are the multitude of flower pot, singing bird, and new moon patterns

HENRY HOUSE — 1769 — NORTH BENNINGTON, VERMONT

that are cut in shutters, wrecking completely the exquisite, soft, velvety texture of the moulded panel. Then, not infrequently, we see a recurrence of the fad of projecting the rafter ends to the underside of the cornice, and, still more, the exotic cut-outs on latticework, the overdoing of shutter fasts, hanging door lamps, queer ironwork, and patterned brick porches and steps, instead of the old, weathered, stone ones or soft, rich, thin bricks laid without mortar.

Bennington, Vermont, and the neighboring towns were on the edge, the frontier of coloniza-

Before entering into a discussion of the characteristics of the Vermont houses, there is one of a more unusual type which demands attention. This is the Henry House at North Bennington, built in 1769 (shown on page 37). The porch, with its square columns, gives an atmosphere unique in houses of the north. Its proportions are generous, the roof lines simple, chimneys good, the detail, especially of the columns, slightly crude. Such little touches as the wooden benches and long slanting leader give an added quaintness. The clapboards are wide and

GOVERNOR GALUSHA HOUSE, SOUTH SHAFTSBURY, VERMONT

tion, while the seacoast towns were quite the center of it. One does not find in these examples the perfection which might have been achieved if they had been in the center of a greater field of activity and experiment, yet several interesting motifs have been developed in Vermont, not to be found in other localities.

The type of house to be found near Bennington seems to be similar to that built in great numbers in the north Connecticut Valley. It is narrow and rectangular in plan. Some are merely box-like structures, but well proportioned with excellent window and door openings.

the corner-boards, as well as the corners of the square columns, have beaded edges. Our modern work often forgets the edges, one of the little refinements which make us enthusiastic and pleased with the old. Analyzing the general scheme we find it a large proportion of gray in the clapboards, a dark space in the shade of the porch relieved by the white of the columns. The doors and windows with the accompanying deep-colored shutters are placed casually, giving an air of comfortable informality.

The Henry House, although of early date, has a more home-like and hospitable atmosphere than some of the later and more typical rectan-

HAWKINS HOUSE, SOUTH SHAFTSBURY, VERMONT

HAWKINS HOUSE, SOUTH SHAFTSBURY, VERMONT

GENERAL DAVID ROBINSON HOUSE, OLD BENNINGTON, VERMONT

gular houses of this section. They were box-like in shape, ornamented at the doors, windows, and cornice. The carpenter-builders became more skillful as they created new structures from year to year, although several houses are very similar.

A detailed triple window has been used over front entrances several times. This form is adapted from the Palladian window and is the unusual feature of some of the houses illustrated in this chapter. Instead of the entablature being placed above the pilasters the central semicircular architrave rests directly on the caps. The remainder of the cap is taken up by the architrave of the smaller arches. The sills return around the plinth and have small moulded brackets supporting the pilasters. Appearing as this motif does three times in the

Detail of Porch

GENERAL DAVID ROBINSON HOUSE, OLD BENNINGTON, VERMONT

houses illustrated, they must have been built by the same carpenter, or else this feature was one of the earliest stock details. The colonial builders always had difficulty in placing such details as Palladian windows because they endeavored to build them into the usual plain front, without considering their relation to the windows on each side. They placed the meeting rail in an awkward manner, making unpleasant divisions of glass. This is an important point, since many good designs are spoiled because panes of different sizes are used throughout a house.

The Palladian window in the Hinsdale House has been regrettably changed by the removal of the original sash. It is not as much in character with the surrounding detail as is the one in the Governor Galusha House at South Shaftsbury,

HOUSE AT WEATHERSFIELD, VERMONT

and yet it in turn is not as interesting as the remarkable window in the house of General David Robinson at Old Bennington. Realizing the weakness of this feature in the Governor Galusha House the carpenter-builder applied pilasters to the main wall of the Robinson House, thereby separating it from the side windows and linking it with the entrance porch.

Studying these three houses, the Hinsdale House is consistent and good in scale, except for the aforementioned triple window. The rich gray most satisfying designs are ones having uniform sizes of glass. The size of glass in the triple window is perfect, and it is regrettable that this size was not used over the entire house. The chimneys are not large enough to be consistent in design with the other details of the house.

The General David Robinson House has the most developed treatment of texture, the strong whites of the porch against the gray of the clapboards, pilasters, and wall, with the exquisitely divided sash softening the dark openings flanked

GALUSHA HOMESTEAD, SOUTH SHAFTSBURY, VERMONT

clapboards, strengthened at the corners by the nicely proportioned quoins capped by the sturdy cornice with delicate dentil-like brackets and relieved by the very simple and rich architraves of the window, denote it as the work of a skillful designer. The door detail is quite in harmony.

Of the Governor Galusha House much might be said about the porch; well might we remember this example when designing for a client who demands a wide generous entrance. Unfortunately the main roof has not its generous spread. The cornice is good in itself but it lacks the feeling of support and the window sash have been changed to panes of a larger glass size. This is unfortunate, for you will find that the by shutters. The detail throughout is delightful in scale. This house is perhaps one of the most beautiful of the examples in this chapter.

A house with a similar *partis* but weak in the duplication of pediments and stronger than the General Robinson House in the pilaster treatment is the Hawkins House at South Shaftsbury. Here, instead of stopping over the front, they carry around and become definite supporting corners to the design. The play of light and shade is masterly, the soft velvety whites of the pilaster, pediment, and window heads, the background of gray and the well-shaped dark openings make it perhaps the most balanced example of texture, but lacking a predominant feature such as exists in the General Robinson House. The double-columned entrance is seldom found, though it might have been more satisfying to have projected the columns farther and separated them slightly to give a deep shaded entrance.

The other two groups, with Palladian windows, with and without pilasters but possessing gable ends, have combined motifs to make the General Robinson House. We then find a third group of rectangular houses with very flat hip

curved brackets, while the Norwich House repeats the window-frieze design very happily in the frieze of the main cornice. The door of this house is perhaps a bit small in size and too intimate in detail, although in itself a most beautiful bit.

As descendants show a likeness to their forebears with here and there a peculiar outcropping of curious characteristics, so in these homes there are the fortunate few having all the refinement of the examples inspiring their chief character-

SAYWOOD HOUSE, WOODSTOCK, VERMONT

roofs, such as the house at Weathersfield, illustrated on page 42, still showing signs of its previous refinement, and the house at Norwich combining characteristics with the Governor Galusha House and the Hawkins House to give us the Leach House at Pawlett, illustrated on page 48. This may not have been what happened, but it was some similar series of events. In the first two Adam details have been used to ornament with frieze over the first-story windows, the Weathersfield House having a door rather common to this type and a boxy cornice with small

istics while occasionally one finds odd off shoots not wholly explainable. There is the long and narrow form represented by the Saywood House at Woodstock, Vermont, with a none too exciting door, while the large and cumbersome type includes the Kneeland House at Hartford, Vermont, illustrated on page 46. The example with the broad tendencies, placing all the interest toward the street, is shown in the illustration on page 43 of another Galusha homestead.

In writing for this chapter an article dealing with texture and color, although the exam-

KNEELAND HOUSE, HARTFORD

HAWKINS HOUSE, SOUTH SHAFTSBURY

TWO DOORWAYS IN VERMONT

ples have been unusually interesting in themselves there has not been the variety quite necessary to illustrate fully the points in discussion. One would have to select from up and down the Atlantic coast to show the variety necessary.

We could start with the Saltonstall-Whipple House (illustrated in Volume IX, Chapter 1, of this series) and the House of the Seven Gables in Massachusetts as examples of clapboard grays, the John Howard Payne and the

grounds, wholly unequaled by any other type of Colonial architecture.

After running through this sequence of development and being analytically inclined one might separate the houses into groups, according to their texture and color values rather than to any peculiarities of plan and construction. The Whipple House might be taken as an example, studied carefully and then compared with the other Colonial houses. Could one possibly mis-

KNEELAND HOUSE, HARTFORD, VERMONT

Anna Halsey houses on Long Island (illustrated in Volume V, Chapter 4) as shingle grays, then a step forward to the clapboard grays with the beautiful divided double-hung sash of early Connecticut work, the addition of shutters and entrance details to the very height of skill in combining grays, whites, and darks as shown in the houses about Litchfield (illustrated in Volume V, Chapter 9), with an attempt at all white in the use of smooth matched siding in the W. H. Sanford House. The Litchfield types have a sparkle, set off by beautiful trees as back-

take it as coming later than the houses mentioned? It would be placed in the period of plain grays, then others in a period of grays and whites, and so on to the later periods of many contrasts and perfect details, with the last group the plain whites. The general effect of the early group is simple and unassuming, while the later is complex and distinguished.

The present day architect is grasping some of the necessary information he must have either to approximate the old or adapt it as we have seen our predecessors do in the several groupings

Entrance Detail
HOUSE AT NORWICH, VERMONT

of the Bennington houses. The requirements of present day home life complicate the composition, and it is only by application and persistence that the designer finally composes a sleeping-porch or persuades an owner that if he has divided upper sash he must have the same in the lower sash. It will be a rocky road for any one who endeavors conscientiously to combine the many desires of the client and at the same time secure for him in the new house the qualities that he unconsciously had admired in the old ones.

LEACH HOUSE, PAWLETT, VERMONT

HOUSE AT NORWICH, VERMONT
See page 47 for entrance detail.

Early Dwellings in
New Hampshire

Text by
A. E. Ferguson
Photographs by
Kenneth Clark
Originally published in 1926 as White Pine Monograph
Volume XII, Number 5

Detail of Entrance
GENERAL REED HOUSE, FITZWILLIAM, NEW HAMPSHIRE

EARLY DWELLINGS IN NEW HAMPSHIRE

AN architectural pilgrimage through New Hampshire reveals the fact that the early settlers did not follow any fixed style in building their houses. There are no characteristics of mass or detail which occur often enough to make it possible to define a "typical" New Hampshire dwelling.

Portsmouth (Strawbery Banke — 1623) and Hampton, the seaport towns, among the first to be settled, attracted a different type of settlers from those colonists who settled the inland towns of Exeter (founded in 1638 by the Reverend John Wheelwright) and Dover (founded by Edward Hilton, sent over from England about 1627), while the farmers sought their fortunes in the fertile valley of the Connecticut. The territory included in the Province of New Hampshire, which from 1638 to 1678 was within the boundaries of Massachusetts, was so large and so sparsely settled that there was small chance for the pioneers to adopt the building traditions of their neighbors. They were little disposed to union among themselves. They came from the other colonies bringing their local architectural traditions with them, and developed these to suit their new environment, producing results which are a constant surprise to the student of early American architecture as he wends his way about the state.

The mansions of Portsmouth are familiar to the readers of this series.* They represent the more sophisticated and elaborate New Hampshire dwelling and were the homes of many of the most distinguished citizens of the late Colonial and early Republican periods.

Owing to the many varieties of religious opinion that prevailed among the radical pioneers, each new grouping and consequent settlement had an individuality all its own, determined by the personality of its leader and the ideas that he represented. The traveler should be prepared to find, therefore, even in the most unexpected places, many examples of early dwellings each with marked individuality. Take, for instance, New Ipswich, settled about 1735, a hamlet uncontaminated by the summer tourist, drowsing its way through the course of time in a beautiful setting of green hills and fertile val-

leys. Here one finds the Laura Hooper House, simple, well proportioned, a farmhouse of the better type, and, near by, the imposing Barrett mansion with stables, outbuildings and all the appurtenances of a colonial "estate." (Mr. Whitehead promises a full and detailed presentation of this house, as it is worthy of a more extended survey than this chapter can give to it.)

The General Reed House, at Fitzwilliam, is a fine example of the well studied composition of the later eighteenth-century period. The nicely proportioned doorway, perfect in detail, the well thought out fenestration and the accent of stability added by the quoins make the ensemble worthy of serious consideration by the modern architect. This house seems to me to be as excellent an example of the "Colonial" as any I have ever seen. Out of the infinite variety of types and styles that make up our early architectural period, this house and a few others similar to it, scattered through the New England section, express the true conception of our pre-Revolutionary builders.

Houses like this one were developed to fit American conditions, life and manners at a time when people had leisure to study how to express the ideals of the American family and hearth in the household arts. The early American styles not only express our ideals, but, as a practical matter, are easy ones in which to design. Their forms are simple, suited to present day methods of construction in contrast with the forms of other styles which are less direct and therefore more costly. They are certainly more appropriate than the pseudo-Spanish and Italian, the lath and plaster "half timber" and other "adoptions" that supply the present day realtor with his stock of "stage-scenery" masquerading as architecture.

The small farmhouse at Westmoreland is an interesting example of the beauty of simplicity. A foursquare, ridge-roof house has been made a lovely piece of architecture by good proportion, fine fenestration and an elaborately moulded doorway, with just a suggestion of rugged ornament that suits so well its background of simple clapboards.

This little town of Westmoreland, by the way, has one of the most beautiful situations in New England. Anyone whose patriotic pride has been dampened by

* "Three-Story Colonial Houses of New England," by Frank Chouteau Brown, Volume IX, Chapter 7; "Portsmouth, New Hampshire, an Early American Metropolis," by Electus D. Litchfield, Volume III, Chapter 3.

a worship of the lovely, rural, English countryside should take the trip to this hamlet, ascend Park Hill and gaze out upon the Connecticut Valley from that eminence. A more perfect picture of rolling hills, winding rivers and all that goes to make up an ideal landscape is seldom found. Were this spot near one of the "tourist centers" of Europe, it would be famed throughout the world. As it is, it is seen by perhaps a half dozen people a year, without counting the local inhabitants who are few and far between.

The Moulton House is a particularly interesting example architecturally, both within and without. Till a year or so ago it was at the crossroads in Hampton, a pathetic structure, slowly disintegrating. It was threatened at any moment with demolition, was then bought by Mr. Harlan G. Little, moved to its present setting and restored most sympathetically. Measured drawings of three of the rooms are shown on pages 62 and 64 of this chapter. The rear has a most interesting gambrel wing, seemingly of a much earlier period than the main house. It was probably the first structure to which the main house was added.

The two houses at Croydon, illustrated on pages 57 and 58, stand side by side in a village of about five houses, and by their juxtaposition accentuate their absolute dissimilarity. The one with the fence and the arched doorway has a certain charm in being based on precedent, the beautiful cornice of the doorway having a more or less classic feeling of design. The Barton House next door is no less charming, but

Map of the Province of New Hampshire
Made in 1777, showing the most inhabited parts

the designer here allowed himself free play and has produced some detail that is original and full of naïveté. The little subfrieze of ornament in the location that is filled by dentils in the usual examples is a startling innovation that justifies itself by the finished results. The planning of a motive above the entrance of almost the same scale and design as the entrance itself is unusual to say the least. But is it not interesting?

These artisans of our early days violated the very rules that present day teachings pronounce necessary to good design, but their finished houses prove how impossible it is to lay down rules for any artistic medium of expression. The inherent good judgment, culture, call it what you will, of some of our early builders was founded on a basis of good taste and an appreciation of proportion that are very difficult to account for when there was no opportunity for architectural education as judged by modern standards. Can the modern farmer-carpenters produce the results that these pioneers obtained? For answer look about you in any "modern" American town. It is written indelibly in the jig-sawed ornaments, the "Gothic" windows and other atrocities that fifty years of Victorian ugliness have left behind.

The period immediately following the War of 1812, except for isolated instances, saw the end of a style of architecture that has never been revived. Although we are on the verge of a renaissance now, the modern architect is just beginning to understand the true motives and subtle characteristics that underlie the work of

FARMHOUSE NEAR WESTMORELAND, NEW HAMPSHIRE

LAURA HOOPER HOUSE, NEW IPSWICH, NEW HAMPSHIRE

GENERAL REED HOUSE, FITZWILLIAM, NEW HAMPSHIRE

their predecessors, and the "Colonial" absurdities of the past decades are giving way to buildings designed by men who through study and knowledge have sensed the beauties of the old work and are incorporating them into their daily practice.

The interior of the house at Claremont and the china closet in the Bellows House at Walpole — while entirely different in feeling and execution — are both fine ex-

has many features that are not in keeping with the earlier work. The tremendous arched window in the pediment is out of scale, yet the general proportions of the façade are good and the brickwork has a lovely texture. The columnar entrances, of which this house has no less than three, are well proportioned and show a lively variation of detail. The wrought iron railing over the front entrance porch adds the finishing touch.

Detail of Entrance
BARTON HOUSE, CROYDON, NEW HAMPSHIRE

amples of the work of their periods. That in Claremont shows a sophistication and a delicacy that are almost Adamesque, while the Bellows china closet, of an earlier period, has an ingenious combination of mouldings, etc., that perhaps will not bear minute analysis, yet in effect the whole is good.

The Swift House of Orford is entirely different from any of the other examples illustrated. It was probably built during the period which began about 1825, as it

The houses illustrated in this chapter were selected from a large collection of interesting examples which have been studied and photographed by the editor and his able collaborators. We are permitted to give but a glimpse of the New Hampshire material which is in store for the readers of this series. We regretfully pass over our task to others who will be more than repaid for their intimate study of these early dwellings, churches and public buildings.

BARTON HOUSE, CROYDON, NEW HAMPSHIRE

Detail of Entrance Doorway
GOODENOUGH HOUSE, CROYDON, NEW HAMPSHIRE

China Closet
JOHN BELLOWS HOUSE, WALPOLE, NEW HAMPSHIRE

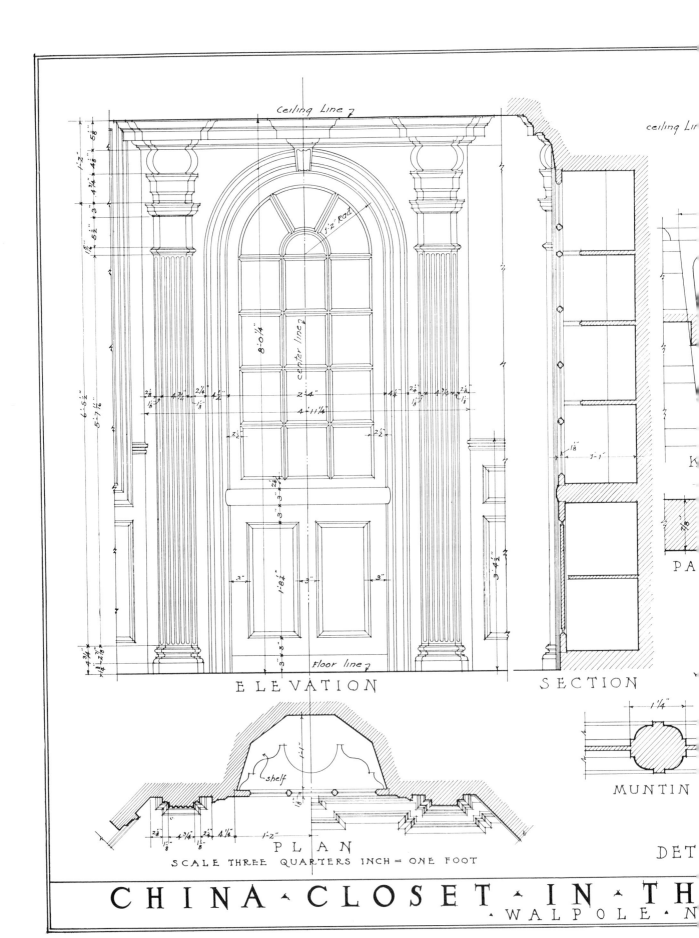

ceiling Line

ceiling Li

1'2" rod

8'0 1/4"

center line

2'4"

4'11 1/4"

1'8 1/2"

floor line

ELEVATION

SECTION

K

PA

shelf

1'4"

MUNTIN

PLAN

DET

SCALE THREE QUARTERS INCH = ONE FOOT

CHINA · CLOSET · IN · TH

· WALPOLE · N

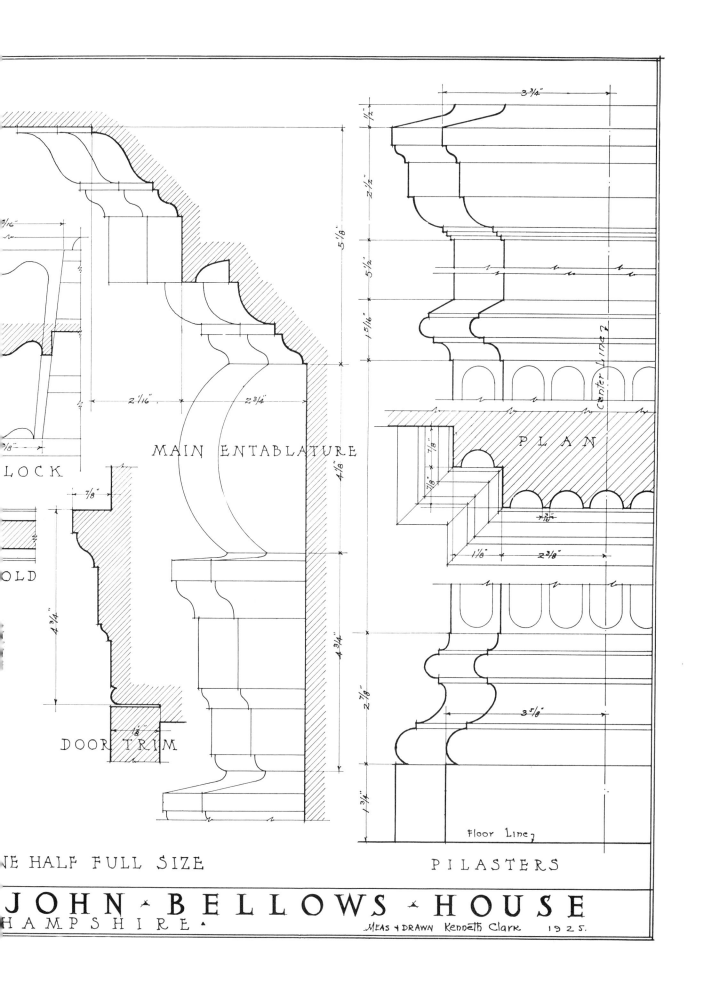

MAIN ENTABLATURE

2'/16".

2 3/4"

5 1/8"

4/8"

4 3/4"

LOCK

7/8"

OLD

4 3/4"

DOOR TRIM

1/8"

3 9/16"

7/8"

3 3/4"

1/2

2 1/2"

5 1/2"

1 5/16"

center Line

P L A N

7/8"

7/8"

7/8"

2 3/16"

1 1/8"

2 3/8"

2 7/8"

3 5/8"

1 3/4"

Floor Line

NE HALF FULL SIZE

PILASTERS

JOHN · BELLOWS · HOUSE

HAMPSHIRE·   MEAS & DRAWN Kenneth Clark   1925.

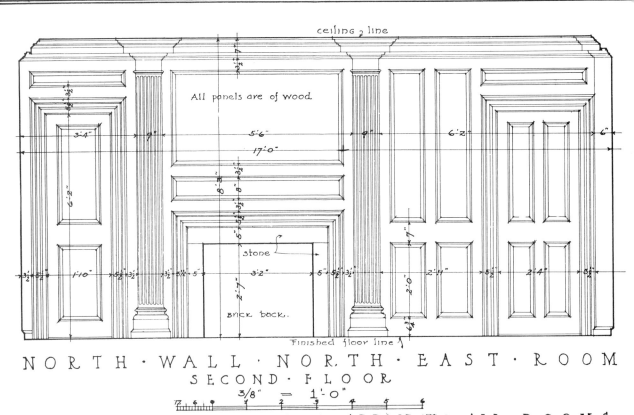

ceiling line

All panels are of wood.

stone

Brick back.

Finished floor line

N O R T H · W A L L · N O R T H · E A S T · R O O M
S E C O N D · F L O O R
3/8" = 1'-0"

½ F U L L · S I Z E · P R O F I L E S · A P P L Y · T O · A L L · R O O M S

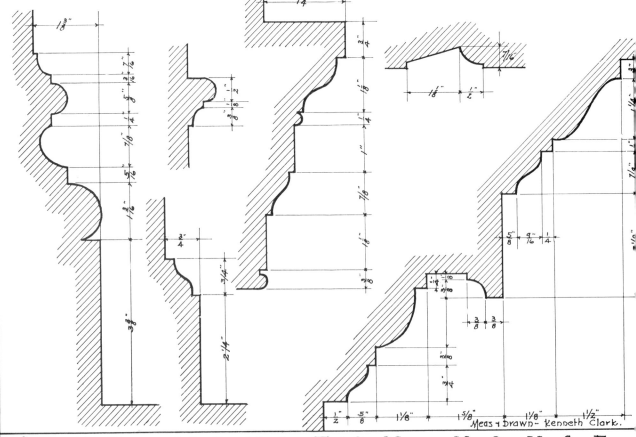

Meas + Drawn — Kenneth Clark.

T H E · M O U L T O N · H O U S E
· H A M P T O N · N E W · H A M P S H I R E ·

GOODENOUGH HOUSE, CROYDON, NEW HAMPSHIRE

GENERAL MOULTON HOUSE, HAMPTON, NEW HAMPSHIRE

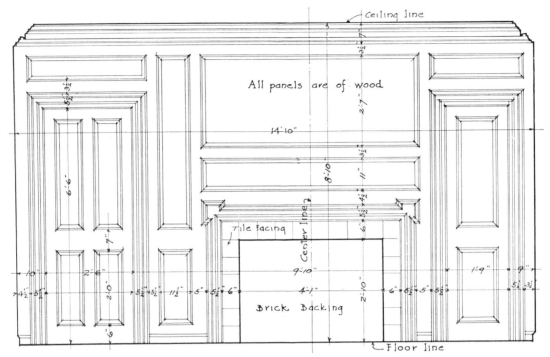

All panels are of wood

Tile facing

Brick Backing

N O R T H · W A L L · S O U T H · E A S T · R O O M
· F I R S T · F L O O R ·

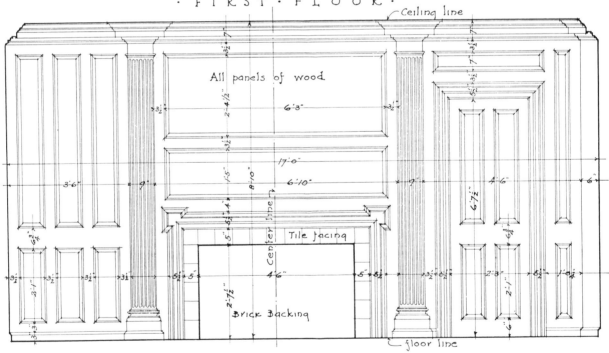

All panels of wood

Tile facing

Brick Backing

N O R T H · W A L L · N O R T H · E A S T · R O O M
· F I R S T · F L O O R ·

S C A L E 3/8" = 1'- 0"

Meas + Drawn Kenneth Clark.

T H E · M O U L T O N · H O U S E
· H A M P T O N · N E W · H A M P S H I R E ·

SWIFT HOUSE, ORFORD, NEW HAMPSHIRE

Detail of Side Doorway
SWIFT HOUSE, ORFORD, NEW HAMPSHIRE

Detail of Front
DEXTER HOUSE, CLAREMONT, NEW HAMPSHIRE

Detail of Parlor
DEXTER HOUSE, CLAREMONT, NEW HAMPSHIRE

Small Colonial Houses

Text by
Peter Augustus Pindar
Photographs by
Kenneth Clark
Originally published in 1931 as White Pine Monograph
Volume XVII, Number 6

HOUSE AT STOWE, MASSACHUSETTS

SMALL COLONIAL HOUSES

IT is not likely that the designers of the small Colonial houses laid such stress upon the design of the exteriors as is today customary. The elevations in almost every case were direct derivatives of the plans and the plans were not, as a rule, conceived with much thought as to their effect on the elevations. In the early houses the informal method of procedure of peasant architecture everywhere in the world was followed: in each locality a certain design proved to be economical in cost, suitable to the living purposes of the colony, and was repeated constantly; became almost a stock design, and variations occurred only in minor items due either to a desire on the part of the owner for some particular sort of ornament or perhaps because the timber happened to cut better to certain sizes than to others.

Houses were of three different heights; of one story, of two stories, and of two stories in the front and one in the rear. In the Dutch colonies they were almost invariably of one story; the roof overhanging the front and rear to a considerable extent but without any eaves on the gable ends. Later, small extensions were made, or in some cases the original house became itself the small extension when a larger house was added to it; so that the rambling picturesque effect of the Dutch house arose from the fact that it was a series of accretions rather than because the designers studied either to change the plan or elevations to procure this picturesque quality.

In Connecticut, the plan used was so stereotyped that it is today known as the Connecticut Plan; that is a small entrance hall about 4' x 6' with a stair crowded in the narrowest possible space between the entrance hall and a central chimney, rooms to the right and left of the entrance hall with fireplaces to the central chimney, and one or two rooms in the rear. This plan was not unusual in other parts of the country, particularly those bordering on Connecticut or settled by Connecticut people. Thus in the eastern end of Long Island we find the houses were almost like those of the Connecticut plan and in certain parts of western New York and southern Ohio, houses of the Connecticut plan were built as late as 1810 and 1815.

In these early houses very respectful attention was paid to the points of the compass, since with the entirely inadequate heating arrangement of the Colonial period, the natural heat of the sun was utilized to its fullest capacity. Thus the Dutch houses almost invariably faced the south and where the roads ran east and west, were parallel with the roads, or as in northern New Jersey, where the roads followed the course of the streams north and south, the gable ends were placed to the highway. It may also be noticed that most of these buildings were placed very close to the road since bad as were conditions on the public highways in early days, the difficulty of keeping up much private road from the highway to the street was so great that it was avoided whenever possible.

The weather was responsible for one feature common to all early houses no matter how unpretentious. They always had entrance halls. Many of our modern small houses have the entrance door directly into the living room: we can afford to lose a little heat every time the door is opened. Our Colonial ancestors could not, and there were invariably no open doorways, but doors that could be closed between this small entrance hall and the living rooms. The kitchen, in which a fire was almost always kept burning, could afford to be on the north, but the living room, where a fire was probably only lighted in the evening, was warmed so much as possible by sunny south west exposures and no conditions of the site were permitted to interfere with this important factor. It made no difference if one had to pass a bedroom or a kitchen to get to the front door if the southern corner happened to be away from the street.

As is indicated above, the plans of all Colonial houses were very generally similar. The existing houses of the smallest type have, as a rule, central entrances with rooms on each side: when the entrance hall is a corner of the house, it is probable that an addition on the other side of the entrance was contemplated at the time that the house was built. Thus in the alteration of old houses with corner entrances, it has been repeatedly found that the chimney back of the stairway had a fireplace built in its base facing and closed by the outside wall so that no alteration of the chimney would be necessary when the addition was built. It will be recalled also that many old houses with corner entrances built of stone or brick, have the gable end next to that corner of clapboards or shingles, indicating that it was regarded as a temporary wall; so that similar in plan as most old houses are, in execution, the contemplated plans were even more alike; and the variety which we discover in the small old houses is due not to any conscious effort on the part of the designers to make them unalike, but rather to the fact that the available materials differed in different localities, that traditional methods of building sprung up and that as families gained in wealth and their needs changed with the times, additions were made often much unlike those originally contemplated.

Possibly the strongest single factor in determining the appearance of the old houses was the roof. In Connecticut and the colonies at the eastern end of Long Island, the salt box roof was the commonest in olden times. It is said that the design of houses of this character was probably suggested by the wooden box in which salt was kept in colonial times, and was common all over New England and New York. Houses of this character illustrated here are the Laws House at Sharon, New Hampshire, the old house at Sturbridge, Massachusetts, and the small house on the green at Milford, Connecticut, (in modified form). The gambrel roof is said to have arisen from an attempt on the part of the colonists to beat the high taxes assessed against two story houses, by making a two story house which technically was a one story house. This tradition is perhaps more picturesque than authentic, but the wide prevalence of these roofs in the colonies as compared with the scarcity of gambrel roofs used in Europe would indicate some specific reason for its introduction: we find it used in various forms in New England, in Maryland, and in New Jersey and New York as, for example, the Hager House, the Dutch house in Englewood and the house in East Hartford, Connecticut.

Of course, the one story house with the straight pitched roof was the commonest of all the early varieties; probably every log hut which antedated the formal building of dressed lumber had a roof of this character, and the tiny examples from Groton, Massachusetts, and Saddle River are illustrative of the type. As time wore on the decorative elements became more important: the architectural orders became almost a necessary part of every respectable dwelling, and were used without much real regard for their appropriateness, purely as decorations just as we alas! sometimes use them today. There is, for example, no real reason

why the street gable end of the house at Stowe, Massachusetts, should be treated with four pilasters supporting the pediment, and as a matter of fact there are good architectural reasons why such a treatment should not be used, as will be seen by examination of the frontispiece. The pilasters have no meaning whatever; there is no reason for the change in material between the sides and the street end; it is in fact, employed simply for its decorative effect; a piece of stage scenery on the street.

The earliest houses were absolutely lacking in porches or piazzas either at the doors or anywhere else. The entrance door, when it was protected at all from the elements, was only protected by the overhang as in the Dutch and early New England houses, or by a deep recess in a stone wall as was the case in Pennsylvania, but later and especially when the Greek Revival had in the minds of the early builders emphasized the architectural treatment, the entrance porches began to play an important part as is well illustrated by the charming little Peyton Randolph House* at Williamsburg, Virginia. The house had a very real architectural quality, and the handsome simple doorway and porch, the pleasant composition of low wings against the small center indicate that plan and elevation grew together in the mind of the designer, as was never the case in the more primitive work.

The emphasis which the colonial architect put on plan and the manner in which he regarded classic ornament as motifs rather than functional features is clearly indicated on the little one story house at Rensselaerville, New York, which has a column on axis in the middle of the front steps with a doorway around the corner to the left. The modern architect would have struggled pretty hard to have his doorway in the center, or failing to adjust his plan to a central doorway, would have modified his motive entirely; not so the early architect. His plan was all right, he got a cover over the porch and he liked the motive. It is the treatment of a cabinet-maker rather than an architect and it is quite likely that much of the early architectural design was done by people who built houses in the summer and made furniture in the winter. We have today a kind of architecture we call decorator's architecture, done by people who have real feeling for ornament and good taste; possibly a genuinely inventive fancy. The results of such architecture are oftentimes more amusing, more interesting than the correct proportions laid out on paper by the practising architect, but they are readily recognizable as the work of amateurs. Much of our most charming Colonial work was obviously the work of amateurs and perhaps that is the reason it is so charming.

*Editor's Note: Subsequent research since the time this monograph was written has revealed that the house illustrated here as Peyton Randolph's is in fact the Semple House or the William Finnie House as it is now listed by Colonial Williamsburg.

HAGER HOUSE—1730—SOUTH SUDBURY, MASSACHUSETTS

LAWS HOUSE—c1800—SHARON, NEW HAMPSHIRE

HOUSE AT 220 GRAND AVENUE, ENGLEWOOD, NEW JERSEY

Built in 1803.

HOUSE AT STURBRIDGE, MASSACHUSETTS

STEUBEN HOUSE, REPUBLIC HILL, PENNSYLVANIA

Cornice Detail
HOUSE ON MAIN STREET, WATERBURY, VERMONT

Cornice Detail
HOUSE AT STOWE, MASSACHUSETTS

SPLOYD HOUSE, RENSSELAERVILLE, NEW YORK

HOUSE ON THE GREEN, MILFORD, CONNECTICUT

PEYTON RANDOLPH HOUSE, WILLIAMSBURG, VIRGINIA

Note: Actually the Semple House or William Finnie House

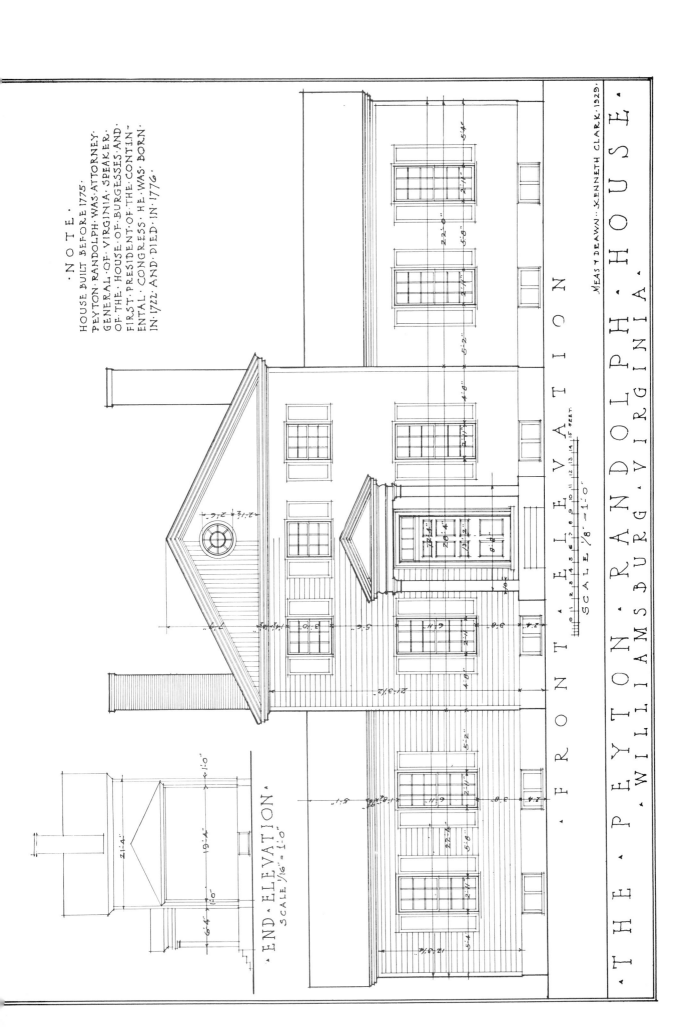

· N O T E ·

HOUSE · BUILT · BEFORE · 1775 ·
PEYTON · RANDOLPH · WAS · ATTORNEY ·
GENERAL · OF · VIRGINIA · SPEAKER ·
OF · THE · HOUSE · OF · BURGESSES · AND ·
FIRST · PRESIDENT · OF · THE · CONTIN ·
ENTAL · CONGRESS · HE · WAS · BORN ·
IN · 1722 · AND · DIED · IN · 1776 ·

· F R O N T · E L E V A T I O N ·

MEAS'? DRAWN ... KENNETH CLARK · 1929 ·

SCALE ⅛" = 1'-0"

· E N D · E L E V A T I O N ·
SCALE ¹/₁₆" = 1'-0"

· T H E · P E Y T O N · R A N D O L P H · H O U S E ·
· W I L L I A M S B U R G · V I R G I N I A ·

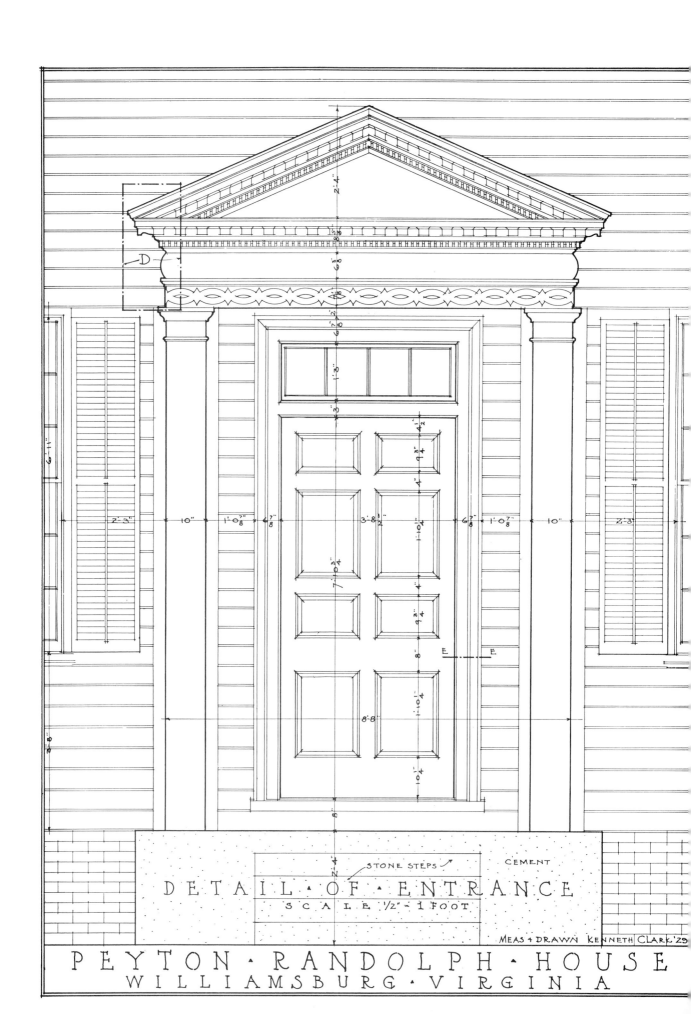

D

STONE STEPS   CEMENT

DETAIL · OF · ENTRANCE
SCALE ½" = 1 FOOT

MEAS & DRAWN KENNETH CLARK '29

PEYTON · RANDOLPH · HOUSE
WILLIAMSBURG · VIRGINIA

COTTAGE AT GROTON, MASSACHUSETTS

Smokehouse
DEMAREST RESIDENCE, SADDLE RIVER, NEW JERSEY

HOUSE AT ORFORD, NEW HAMPSHIRE

HOUSE AT EAST HARTFORD, CONNECTICUT

Detail of Entrance Porch
HOUSE AT DOVER PLAINS, NEW YORK

SMALL COLONIAL HOUSE ON THE OLD BOSTON POST ROAD

ROUND HOUSE, SOUTHWICK'S GROVE, MIDDLETOWN, RHODE ISLAND

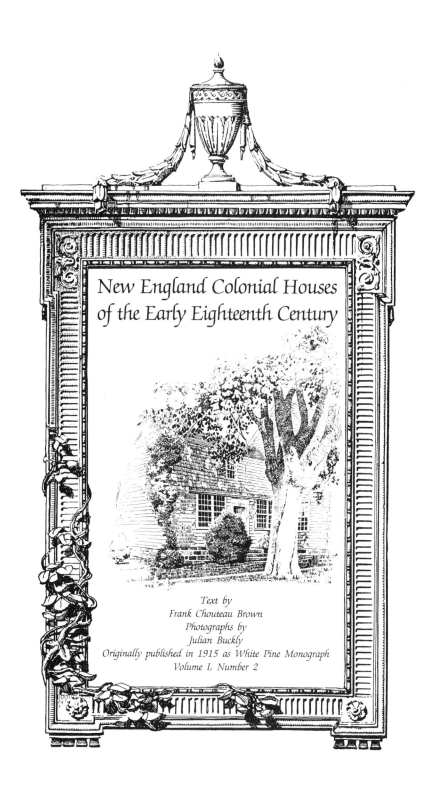

New England Colonial Houses
of the Early Eighteenth Century

Text by
Frank Chouteau Brown
Photographs by
Julian Buckly
Originally published in 1915 as White Pine Monograph
Volume I, Number 2

ISAAC ROYALL HOUSE, MEDFORD, MASSACHUSETTS

The east front, now facing the street. Built in 1732 along the lines of a "nobleman's house" in Antigua. An unusual feature is the horizontal emphasis obtained from the treatment of the windows.

NEW ENGLAND COLONIAL HOUSES OF THE EARLY PORTION OF THE EIGHTEENTH CENTURY

THE early architecture of New England is, for the most part, distinctive for its simplicity and economy, both of plan and construction. It was based, in the first instance, upon rooms of small size and low height, and was as easy to erect and furnish as to heat and defend from enemies, climatic and human. The construction was a simple framework, whose principal supports—generally either of oak or white pine—were hewn from native timber and framed in the fashion the early colonists previously had been accustomed to in England. These timbers were also spaced with an economy in use that permitted the spaces between to be spanned with small irregular pieces of timber and boarding; just as the non-supporting partitions were, in turn, most frequently composed of roughly shaped plank. These heavy timbers once settled into place, the walls could be strengthened against arrows or cold by a further protective filling of brick or tile, so often disclosed when old dwellings are torn down. In one place only was the scale invariably ample and generous; and this was around the central chimney, always the feature of the house.

In the early Colonial cottage again, little, if any, attempt was made for mere ornament or decoration. Recollections of European craftsmanship were adapted to new conditions with little

Entrance Detail

Front Elevation

DOAK HOUSE, MARBLEHEAD, MASSACHUSETTS

apparent trouble, and with what we now realize to have been greatly successful common sense. When these structures have remained unaltered by succeeding generations, they are rarely anything but beautiful in their direct outlines and sturdy proportions; the composition of skyline and chimney with the ground contour, and the grouping and proportions of the wall openings being always notably successful. Occasionally these early carpenters, in an entrance doorway, a mantel, or perhaps in the staircase, would seize the chance to apply their craft-knowledge with a little more freedom from restraint, and while the results may sometimes seem to us perhaps a bit *naïve* or quaintly obvious, at other times one cannot help but acknowledge they display as superb an acquaintance with, and appreciation of, beauty in line, detail and in the placing and modeling of ornament as any inventions of other and more sophisticated days.

The earliest type of plan had undoubtedly a room on each side of an entrance, a staircase placed in front of a central chimney, and a kitchen, located perhaps partly in a rear shed or ell.

Such an arrangement is ordinarily regarded as of the farmhouse type, and is sufficiently familiar hardly to require illustration. If such is to be supplied, a typical example is found in the Cushing House at Hingham, or the old Tyler House at Wayland, standing on the old prehistoric Indian "Bay Path." This latter house dates from the early part of the eighteenth century (sometime previous to 1725) and is now deserted. At the rear the roof of this house now sweeps down, nearly to the ground, in the usual fashion, being unbroken for any purposes of light or ventilation. As originally built, the house undoubtedly consisted of four rooms only: two below and two above. As it now stands, the kitchen runs the full width of the ell, and is located exactly in the center, behind the chimney, with a small room behind the front room on the left of the entrance: the space at the right being taken up by closets and the side entrance. The original frame is of hewn oak, covered with one thickness of weatherboards beveled on

Detail of Window
JUDGE JOSEPH LEE HOUSE, CAMBRIDGE, MASSACHUSETTS

the edges to overlap without lathing or plastering, but with the timber frame filled in with soft burned brick. Another indication of the age of this house is the abrupt overhang or projection at the eaves line, without soffit moulding or any other suggestion of the later cornice treatment.

There are to be found only a very few instances of a house of interestingly different type, where the chimney and staircase occur at one end instead of in the center, leaving but one room across the front. Such a type appears in the little Southborough house, where the typical projected face-gable showing at the end indicates how naturally the early builders adapted their plan to get the outlook and sun desired in rear rooms.

In this house there existed a curious detail of

A GOOD EXAMPLE OF AN EARLY FARMHOUSE, NEAR BOSTON, MASSACHUSETTS
Illustrating shingle ends combined with clapboarding on the front.

construction in the window-caps, intended to protect the top of the window-case, which was projected beyond the frame of the building and applied to its face in the old-fashioned way. These moulded caps were crowned by a sloping member, carefully hewn and shaped from one heavy log of wood so as to provide a sloping "wash" across the top and front and returned on the two ends; while the carpenter took pains to leave a standing flange at the back over which the siding was broken, thus providing a sort of flashing, but executed entirely in wood!

Later in the eighteenth century, the American builders began to secure the "Carpenter's Handbooks," first published in England about 1756, and from these they developed new details far

Front Door
SHUTE HOUSE, HINGHAM, MASSACHUSETTS

more easily, merely adapting them to the somewhat simplified conditions and requirements of the American village or town in which they lived and worked. Later, the demand for these practical builders' assistants became so great that al least one volume was reprinted in this country; being compiled and issued by a certain Asher Benjamin, an architect in Greenfield, Massachusetts, in 1797.

For a number of years the plan developed few changes, except in so far as they were demanded by special or larger requirements imposed by the owner. The house on page 94 is of this simple type, save that it presents the less usual composition of one window on one side the center door balanced by two upon the other; the single window being four lights wide

JOHN DOCKRAY HOUSE, WAKEFIELD, RHODE ISLAND
Built in the early part of the eighteenth century.

TYLER HOUSE—BEFORE 1725—WAYLAND, MASSACHUSETTS
A typical example of a farmhouse with a room on each side of entrance and a central chimney.

CUSHING HOUSE, HINGHAM, MASSACHUSETTS
Built in the early part of the eighteenth century, probably in 1730; a good example of the simple farmhouse type.

BEMIS HOUSE — c1750 — WATERTOWN, MASSACHUSETTS

STEARNS HOUSE, BEDFORD, MASSACHUSETTS
Built from a design by Reuben Duren, Architect.

(or twenty panes in all) where the others are of three wide, or fifteen lights.

A very ancient house indeed was the old Doak House at Marblehead, which unfortunately has disappeared. Aside from the simplicity—almost the crudity—of the execution of its architectural details, the age of his building is evidenced by many other indications only to be recognized by the architect or antiquarian. Nevertheless, its definite attitude of dignity, of aloofness, should be apparent to any passerby, and it is this quality, sometimes, as much as any other, that arouses our admiration for these early Colonial masterpieces. They achieve so perfect, if unconscious, a relations of parts—the proportion of opening to wall space and of glass division; the architraves around the opening to window area; the cornice to the roof design and the wall height —that it often seems impossible to improve the structure as a whole. Even though single details sometimes appear crudely executed by local workmen, it yet remains an open question whether mere improvement in execution or in refinement —if attempted—would be as well related, and harmonize as well with the complete design.

The gambrel roof type— always difficult to proportion —was used by the early builders with the greatest freedom, and with a perfect sense for the right relation of parts. Sometimes the gambrel is flattened and ample in proportion, at others the gable appears more restricted and the proportions made for greater dignity and height. It is this latter aspect that is more appropriately found on the larger houses to which this variation of the roof of Mansart was occasionally applied, although undoubtedly it was then, as now, best adapted to enlarge the living space available on the second floor.

The Wadsworth House, sometimes called the President's House, on the grounds of Har-

vard University, while of much larger size— crowding three stories and an attic under its capacious roof beams—has a gambrel of very nearly the proportion of the modest cape cottages. The walls of this house were "raised" on May 24, 1726, although the side doorway, the ell, and the two one-story additions made on each end are of later dates.

In the very well known Royall House in Medford were, besides the slave quarters and the portion shown in the photographs, two ells, one of which may have been the earlier farmhouse that stood upon this site. One of these ells was burned only a few years ago. It is supposed that the original farmhouse built here by Governor Winthrop, soon after the settlement of Medford in 1630, was incorporated into the dwelling later built by John Usher, after he came into possession of the place in 1677.

Despite its unaccustomed surroundings, the Shirley-Eustis Home in Roxbury stands, only slightly removed from its original site, as dignified today as when it was first built. An old newspaper of 1865 proclaiming a sale of the house's contents gives the date as 1743; and adds the information that it was built of oak framed in England and of imported brick—although three different sizes are now to be found. The house was purchased by Governor Eustis in 1819, and it may be that he added the two porches at either end which have now disappeared, but which were so seldom found on early houses in the New England colonies. This house also has two fronts; and, as in the Royall House, the driveway front again proves to be of the more interest architecturally.

Although a little later than the middle of the century, the Shute House at Hingham is so interesting a type as to require consideration here. The lot was bought in 1754 and the house built by 1762, and the ell is of later date.

FARMHOUSE, SOUTHBOROUGH, MASSACHUSETTS

WOOD·CAP
Flashing·edge
Front view Section of End
Angle of Cap
Sketch of Old Windows House at SOUTHBOROUGH Mass
Frank·Chouteau Brown Del 15
Boarding
Clap·boards
Wood Cap
Head
Sill

Front Elevation

Side Elevation

WADSWORTH HOUSE — 1726 — CAMBRIDGE, MASSACHUSETTS

The way the front clapboards extend by and beyond the clapboarding across the
end gable, without corner boards or other finish of any kind, should be noted.

Entrance Detail

WADSWORTH HOUSE—1726—CAMBRIDGE, MASSACHUSETTS

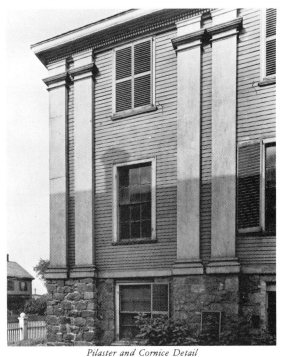

Pilaster and Cornice Detail

SHIRLEY-EUSTIS HOUSE—c1750—ROXBURY, MASSACHUSETTS

SHIRLEY-EUSTIS HOUSE, ROXBURY, MASSACHUSETTS

Built by Governor Shirley, about 1750. This house has two fronts—the principal one
originally facing the water; the south-side fronts upon the driveway turn and approach.

West Doorway
"THE LINDENS" — 1745 — DANVERS, MASSACHUSETTS

Front Doorway
HOUSE — c1760 — HINGHAM, MASSACHUSETTS

ISAAC ROYALL HOUSE — 1732 — MEDFORD, MASSACHUSETTS

A small part of this house, built in 1631, is the oldest section of any house now standing in America. The principal portion of the mansion was not, however, built until 1732. The exterior of the front and back of this house is in the original white pine.

Entrance Detail
ROYALL HOUSE — 1732 — MEDFORD, MASSACHUSETTS
This door opened on the carriage court yard, facing toward the old summerhouse.

SHUTE HOUSE, HINGHAM, MASSACHUSETTS

Detail of Side Entrance
SHUTE HOUSE, HINGHAM, MASSACHUSETTS
A house of unusual type, built about 1762.

Three-Story Colonial Houses
of New England

Text by
Frank Chouteau Brown
Photographs by
Julian Buckly
Originally published in 1917 as White Pine Monograph
Volume III, Number 1

Detail of Entrance

CROWNINSHIELD HOUSE—1798–1803—DANVERSPORT, MASSACHUSETTS

The chaste simplicity and beauty of this entrance doorway and window overhead are well indicated in this picture. Indeed, of all the three-story houses produced in this section, this dwelling seems to be the most perfectly proportioned, and at the same time the simplest, example.

THREE-STORY COLONIAL HOUSES OF NEW ENGLAND

EDITOR'S NOTE: This article was a part of the original manuscript on "New England Colonial Houses" contributed by Mr. Brown for the previous chapter. Because of the quality and quantity of the illustrations which had been collected and the limited space available in a single issue in which to present them, the material was more closely classified and one chapter devoted to the smaller houses of early date and another to the three-story dwellings as herewith shown.

THE Colonial dwellings of New England group themselves naturally into three definite physical classifications. There is first the small cottage one story and a half high, an early and more primitive type found in the smaller and less wealthy communities or in the country. This kind of cottage is typical of certain sections, such as part of Maine and Cape Cod; and certain fisher villages, such as Biddeford Pool, Marblehead, portions of Gloucester and other towns. Some of these cottages are essentially charming, but they possess little value except the incidental detail for most architectural work of the current day.

There is, secondly, the larger house of two stories and roof, containing generally an attic story. This house may be of the simplest possible type of pitch roof with end gable, typical of the larger farmstead; or, in order to provide more space on the third floor, the gable may be developed in the familiar gambrel roof. Or, this same type of house may itself easily extend into the larger, more spacious and pretentious abode of the landed proprietor, wealthy merchantman or shipowner, where we find the most beautiful architectural details that, for delicacy, refinement and restraint, have not elsewhere been equaled under any other conditions on this continent and never surpassed.

In New England there was little tendency to develop the type of mansion familiar throughout the South. The central house with extended wings on both sides is rarely found, except in some uncommon instances, such as the Black House at Ellsworth, or the Governor Gore mansion outside of Boston. On the other hand, the unbalanced development of a big house with one wing is very often seen, particularly in such sections, for instance, as the Old Providence Plantations, or in Salem, or wherever considerable wealth had come into the possession of the leading merchants or families of that time. In these more crowded and larger colonial cities, however, this wing extension generally developed at the back of the main house — rather than extended parallel with the street frontage — and there it often grew until it produced a well-defined enclosure surrounding a servants' court yard at the back or one side of the main house. This tendency is definitely indicated in the Royall House, and even more clearly in some of the old Providence and Portland houses, or the Pierce-Nichols House at Salem, for instance. While the New England mansion of this type developed many interesting details of handling, its general exterior architectural treatment remained nevertheless fairly balanced and formal, and, within the rigid outlines prescribed by custom, no very great variation of design or *parti* was possible. It therefore came naturally to be that, when in New England a still larger dwelling was demanded by conditions, it rather took the form of the three-story house than attempted to extend a second ell or wing to balance the one formerly thrown out — and this type of dwelling, possessing peculiar architectural difficulties of its own for solution, came soon to be recognized as a third principal, characteristic type that distinguished some of the later houses of New England that were generally built just previous to, or immediately after, the year 1800. That the type was not exclusively to be found in any one locality is proved by the accompanying illustrations, which have been selected purposely to illustrate the considerable geographical area from which the material was drawn, and have intentionally avoided reproducing any of the

the entrance was published. This house was built in 1760 and was very soon after increased by the addition of the third story in a treatment that on its architectural side, by the way, is sufficiently simple and direct to be quite convincing.

The problem of undertaking to increase the Colonial house to three stories in height and retain its usual and nearly square proportions in plan, is one that might well cause the architectural designer to pause and carefully regard the difficulties presented by the problem of

HAVEN HOUSE — c1800 — PORTSMOUTH, NEW HAMPSHIRE

The porch and doorway, window caps and cornice help to relieve the squareness of the design.

most familiar and well-known three-story structures in Salem, or selecting more than one or two of the most important or suggestive examples from Portsmouth, Portland, or the other larger New England communities.

In this connection it is perhaps instructive to refer to two other chapters, one containing the Isaac Royall House at Medford (Chapter 6), which is distinctly of a foreign and more palatial three-story type, suggesting the Southern treatment of the central building with wings, which dates from as early as 1732; and the other recalling the Bishop Apthorp House in Cambridge (Chapter 8), of which only a detail of

making such a box-like structure attractive and consistent with his Colonial ideals. Such a square and uncompromising house as the old Haven homestead at Portsmouth, for instance, contains little architectural relief from its rectangular proportions except such as is to be found in the caps of the windows, the delicate arched detail of the very broad and overhanging cornice, and the balustrade, that, in the case of the porch at least, has every suggestion of being a more modern addition to the design. Here the original builders evidently felt that they could do no less than make a virtue of necessity and so give to the porch and doorway all the emphasis of dignity and height that the house façade made possible, their only attempt at diminishing the height being found in the low third-story windows, only two panes of glass high.

The Woodbury mansion near Portsmouth indicates a more conscientious endeavor to relieve the box-like exterior proportions of the dwelling by the horizontal bands, the increase in height of the first and second story windows, and the balconies used across the front. Again, dignity and simplicity, with great refinement

ment and simplicity in design and proportion. Seen as it appears in these photographs, without blinds or shutters, and largely minus paint, it nevertheless commands attention and respect from these very sterling qualities of a majestic consciousness of innate beauty and serenity of proportion and refinement detail.

Rather earlier in date than most of these other houses (as indicated by its bold and virile moulding section and heavy window caps) is "Elmwood" in Cambridge. With the fenestration rather more gracefully composed, and with only

GOVERNOR WOODBURY MANSION, NEAR PORTSMOUTH, NEW HAMPSHIRE

Built in 1809 by Captain Samuel Ham. Purchased by Levi
Woodbury (Governor of New Hampshire 1823–1824) in 1839.

of proportion, are indicated—particularly in the details of the porch, where the balustrade is even more obviously a modern addition, although the roof balustrade with its halved balusters seems more consistently to belong to the original design. This house is greatly favored by setting in a rather beautiful grove, where the unkempt terraces and tree surroundings add greatly to its interest and attractiveness.

At Danversport still stands an old house, much battered by wind and weather in its exposed location, of less depth in plan than is usual with the three-story house, and with far more than the usual chaste beauty of refine-

what adventitious and incidental element of balance is obtained from the porch on one side and the one-story service wing on the other, this house ventures sturdily to win approbation solely by means of the rather unusual treatment of entrance and second-story window overhead, —which, in its present form at least, is largely a conjectural reproduction of what may have been its original design.

One of the most unusually interesting—and also surprisingly little known—houses near Boston is the Baldwin House at Woburn, which is in some ways more pretentious and elaborate in treatment and detail than any other example of the three-story type to be found in the general vicinity of Boston. The siding of this house is entirely treated in imitation of the effect of stone divisions; the corner pilasters are given an entasis that is more nearly a "belly"; the architraves impinge upon a delicately moulded cornice; the roof balustrade is typical, in the refinement of its baluster shape and halving, of its comparatively old period; and finally, the entrance feature and Palladian window—while the former is somewhat injured by its extra

cap design is here laid aside for a sturdy and bold virility that is, under the circumstances, rather surprising. In this particular case an incidental defect is noted in the fact that, some time or other, the front columns of the entrance porch have been replaced by crudely turned shafts, and the bases of the former fluted columns have been utilized in place of the presumably exposed capitals. The balustrade here goes back to a break in the roof that suggests a monitor deck treatment: rather a more con-

CROWNINSHIELD HOUSE, DANVERSPORT, MASSACHUSETTS

Built by Nathan Reed between 1798, when he purchased this part of Governor Endicott's old Orchard Farm, and 1803, when he finished his term in Congress. The house was afterward owned by Captain Crowninshield and Captain Benjamin Porter. In the pond in front of the dwelling the first owner experimented with a paddle-wheel steamboat.

width and both are in detail and size better suited to a two-story than a three-story type of house—yet remain nevertheless so interesting and suggestive for the architect as to make it nearly unique in importance among the treatments of this type of house to be found in New England.

At North Andover is an example of a McIntire three-story house less well known than the example in Salem itself. McIntire, when working on a house of this type, evidently followed his book very closely for his proportions and details—the well-known refinement of his carving in mantelpieces and gateposts and door-

sistent and plausible location for this mode of roof adornment. The fenceposts of the gate at the rear of the house were brought from Salem to their present location, and are—as was of course to be expected!—also attributed to the much over-worked and omnipresent Samuel McIntire himself.

The John Pierce House at Portsmouth is one of the well-known examples of this type of structure; and, despite the abominable entrance porch, its chaste simplicity and beauty of detail and moulding ornamentation amply serve to retain its interest for the student of good architecture.

Detail of Front

"ELMWOOD," RESIDENCE OF JAMES RUSSELL LOWELL, CAMBRIDGE, MASSACHUSETTS

The door itself is of recent inspiration, and some parts of the entrance feature are executed in new woodwork. How far they exactly reproduce the original, it is of course impossible to determine. This photograph clearly shows the omission of corner-boards and treatment of siding at the angles.

"ELMWOOD," RESIDENCE OF JAMES RUSSELL LOWELL, CAMBRIDGE, MASSACHUSETTS

This house is supposed originally to have been built (in what was then old Watertown) either by John Stratton in 1760 or by Colonel Thomas Oliver in 1770 or 1780. One of the latter dates appears the more probable. The one-story addition shown at the left is of recent date.

KITTREDGE HOUSE, NORTH ANDOVER, MASSACHUSETTS

Attributed to Samuel McIntire, and very similar to the design of the Pierce-Nichols House in Salem, built by him in 1780 or 1782. The same heavy detail and corner pilaster treatment are found in both structures.

Simplest—and most beautiful—of all the houses of this type is the Boardman House at Portsmouth. Evidently the designer had merely in mind to carry out a design such as had been elsewhere used on a brick façade, substituting plank boarding for the other material, and at the same time greatly beautifying his whole composition by the charming grade, attenuation and refinement of the columns and pilasters in the curved porch and recessed Palladian window motif overhead. Such delicacy of moulding treatment and simplicity of design as are here shown would hardly be consistent with the heavier material and the larger scale of a brick dwelling—but as it is, this house remains perhaps the most beautiful, chaste and distinguished instance of the Puritan treatment of this type of dwelling to be found in the New England colonies, and so should serve as epilogue and apogee to this brief record and appreciation of a type of Colonial dwelling unique and restricted to this section of North America.

COLONEL LOAMMI BALDWIN HOUSE, WOBURN, MASSACHUSETTS

The owner was an important and influential officer in the early colonies and the discoverer and improver of the Baldwin apple. The half-balusters and odd belly on the corner pilasters, along with their awkward height relation to the windows, are all to be noted in this view.

Detail of Entrance

COLONEL LOAMMI BALDWIN HOUSE, WOBURN, MASSACHUSETTS

The very delicate detail shown in this picture and the small scale of the rusti-
cated boarding seem inconsistent with the width of the entrance feature
and the size of the whole house. The glass division is novel and unusual.

JOHN PIERCE HOUSE—1799—COURT STREET, PORTSMOUTH, NEW HAMPSHIRE

This house contains an excellent example of the old-fashioned circular staircase. The porch is a regrettable later addition. This design has been attributed by some to Bulfinch.

BOARDMAN HOUSE, PORTSMOUTH, NEW HAMPSHIRE

Built by Langley Boardman, an expert cabinet-maker, about 1800. The front hall, which was prepared in 1816, shows scenes from Sir Walter Scott's "Lady of the Lake" and still appears in excellent condition. The front is treated with plain siding.

Detail of Entrance Porch and Doorway

LANGLEY BOARDMAN HOUSE, PORTSMOUTH, NEW HAMPSHIRE

Although the beauty of detail of the Palladian window does not appear in this photograph, it shows at least the delicacy, grace and beauty of the attenuated porch columns, and the refinement of the detail in the cornice above and in the equally refined mahogany door with its delicately moulded panels.

Late Eighteenth Century
Architecture in Massachusetts

Text by
Julian Buckly
Photographs by
Julian Buckly
Originally published in 1916 as White Pine Monograph
Volume II, Number 2

Detail of Entrance Doorway
HOUSE — c1800 — WAYLAND, MASSACHUSETTS
The trellis and seats are new, having been added by Ralph Adams Cram, Architect, the present owner and occupant.

ARCHITECTURE IN MASSACHUSETTS DURING THE LATTER PART OF THE EIGHTEENTH CENTURY

OUTSIDE of that very early and almost conjectural colony house type that at first reflected far more of the aspect of its English Gothic predecessor than it hinted at the lighter form of classical dwelling, there was also the early and unpretentious "farmhouse." It was doubtless because of its simple and economical lines that this type persisted for so many years — even, as a matter of fact, until this very day — although its late derivatives are, unfortunately, so deficient in all its original inherent attributes of beauty of proportion and delicacy and refinement of moulding and scale as scarcely to permit the relationship to be now recognizable.

So these earlier dwellings, which were generally of the very simplest pitch-roof type — the low shed, with its eaves hardly above the ground at the back, being in the most part a later addition — continued to reappear, for well over a hundred years, as the houses of the "first settlers" in new communities, springing up along the New England coast and its inland river valleys. They also persisted, till a much later time, as the "farmhouse" *par excellence* throughout all New England.

To cover the development thoroughly, it is perhaps necessary further to speak of the houses of the humbler families, or those built in the more sparsely settled communities, and in those sections where the men were fisherfolk or the farms sterile or sandy. Here a still simpler kind of cottage, of one story, with a low-pitched or gambrel roof, was simultaneously developing in use; but this "cottage type" is so architecturally distinct and separate a form that its consideration here would but serve to confuse the reader interested in tracing the development of New England Colonial architecture — and so, having been mentioned, it will be left until it can be fully and separately studied by itself.

To resume, this simple pitch-roof, farmhouse type, one room deep and two stories high, was at first built exclusively with one ridge pole and two end gables, making the simplest possible form of roof, unbroken by dormers, as it then provided only an unfinished attic space meagrely lighted from the gable ends. The pitch of this roof varied greatly. A few very early examples show the steeper pitch of Gothic influence. Later it lowered naturally to more nearly the Georgian proportion; though there can be no doubt but that the builders of these simple houses were more concerned to get just that exact relation where the pitch was steep enough to throw off the water from its shingled slopes, with the use of the minimum factor of safety, while it would still be low enough to permit of the use of the shortest and smallest rafter lengths allowed by a due regard for these practical requirements, than to display any regard for, or perhaps even knowledge of, the classic precedent that had then recently become customary and established in England. But the roof pitch continued gradually to flatten as time went on — a process in which the kind of roof with two slopes, known generally as gambrel, may somewhat have assisted — until at last, well into the nineteenth century — 1830 or 1840, or thereabouts — it arrived at the low slope appropriate to the revival of the Greek influence that, when first blending with its predecessor, produced such beautiful and dignified results.

But as this very simple yet beautiful farmhouse type did not always satisfy the needs of those communities that were, by the end of the eighteenth century, growing decidedly more prosperous, developing a wealthy class that in their turn at once demanded more pretension and style in their dwellings while being willing and able to expend more money upon them, both the plan and the architectural style of these houses began rapidly to change. In plan the house first grew a service ell that extended more and more, as the prosperity of the farm grew, until it often ran slam into the big barn itself. This was the almost invariable method on the farm, where land was plenty and the living requirements of the family itself changed but little from generation to generation.

Detail of Entrance
FARMHOUSE, MILTON, MASSACHUSETTS
The pilasters are an excellent example of chisel carving.

Sometimes this ell grew on at the rear, sometimes it extended at the side, sometimes it grew in two parts (then generally termed "wings") extending either to right and left of the old house, or, less frequently, running back from each side or end, making the E-shape plan.

In the colonial village or town, however, so simple an "addition" met neither the needs nor conditions that were most likely to exist. Land was more restricted and expensive, and, what was quite as important, the growing social amenities of family life required more than the old two-room first-story plan. It is true that at first it was possible to retain one of these rooms as a parlor and turn the old dining room into a separate living room, building a new dining room and

FARMHOUSE — c1800 — MILTON, MASSACHUSETTS
An unusual element occurs in the old porch and in the projection of the first-story rooms.

kitchen at the rear in an ell. But this was merely an emergency measure, perhaps necessary in temporarily fixing over the old house. When the time to build a new one arrived, the two-room plan of the old farmhouse was exactly doubled: the center hall was continued through the house and two more rooms were built at the back, one upon either side. Thus a parlor, living room, dining room and kitchen were provided on the first floor; and, as the need of a library or office came to be felt, the old method of adding a new kitchen in an ell was again resorted to; and once again the plan began to develop and grow in this same way, following much the same natural process, it should be observed, as Nature has herself ordained for the growth of the pollywog!

So, too, the exterior underwent changes at the same time. The double depth of the house —making it nearly square in plan—ran the old pitched roof and end-gabled ridge pole so high into the air as at once to introduce new possibilities. Either its steep pitch could be retained and the old unused attic be utilized as a third living floor—an opportunity much needed by some of the very generous families accruing to the early settlers!—or the appearance of the house could be obviously helped by again re-

ducing the rafter length (a practical and economical aspect natural to these early builders), thus lowering at once both the ridge and pitch of the roof. This produced an end gable that perhaps appeared rather awkward in proportion to the colonial carpenter's eye, trained to a steeper slope; and so he probably at once thought of the possibility of pitching his roof from all four rather than from only two sides, and the newer, more prosperous and capacious square Colonial house type was born!

Typical of the "farmhouse" group is the old red house in Milton, now a part of the large Russell Farm; and while its exact date is not known, it is supposed to have been built some time before 1800, by one Nathaniel Robbins, and is distinguished from most of its associates by an unusual architectural feature in the two projecting one-storied portions occurring on both ends. Although from the outside these might seem to be later additions to an older house, internally they have every appearance of having been built at the same time as the rest of the structure. The cornice and dado finish continue around the rooms without break, while inside the room does not show the break that outside allows the corner-board to continue down and the projecting ell cornice to

Photograph by Wilfred A. French

GENERAL PUTNAM HOUSE—c1744—DANVERS, MASSACHUSETTS
The outer vestibule and railing are carpenter additions.

Detail of Pilaster
HOOPER HOUSE, HINGHAM, MASSACHUSETTS

butt against it, both refinements displaying some evident skill and forethought on the part of the builder. The difference is made up in thickness of walls; the main house front wall being furred-in to effect this purpose, as well as to provide cheeks to take care of the inside window shutters in the window reveals.

It is impossible to give a date to the porch. Its unusually simple detail and close relation to the old extension give every assurance of its being contemporaneous, despite the fact that it is so rare a feature of colonial work. The doorway is crude and archaic in some of its chiseled carpenter-carved decoration, but all the more interesting for that. Whether built at an earlier date or not, this house could easily pass as from twenty-five to fifty years older than the date assigned it above.

The Emery House at Newburyport, built by Thomas Coker in 1796, is an unusually clear example of the simply planned front house with the added rear ell. In this case the front part has a gambrel roof, of exactly perfect proportions, and the ell a simpler pitched roof, as is often found when the ell's narrower width brings the two rafters of the same pitch as the lower slope of the gambrel to a ridge intersection occurring at the same point where the gambrel's upper flatter slope begins. The outside vestibule entrance, at the place indicated, is unusual; and the vestibule, while, as usual, of later date, is a good example of its kind. In

fact, much of the bare appearance of this house is occasioned merely by its lack of blinds.

Another very similar example of the gambrel roof type is the General Putnam House in Danvers—in its present state representing approximately the period of 1744 (although a claim has been advanced that a portion of the house is as old as 1648). This house has, in addition to its low ell, a comparatively modern vestibule with a characteristically modern carpenter's version of a balustrade above it. This house presents as much of a contrast as is possible to the Dalton House at Newburyport. While variously dated as being built from 1750 to 1760, the photograph of this house speaks for itself, presenting an unusually spacious and generous treatment of the gambrel roof slope (now slated, while the house has a new end bay and suspiciously widely spaced columns at the entrance!). The whole design nevertheless shows much more refinement of handling than is apparent in the other example mentioned.

The Dummer House at Byfield, near Newburyport, is a less well known example of a prim New England type, of which the Warner House at Portsmouth is perhaps the best known existing structure. As in the latter case, it frequently has the brick ends that follow naturally from dividing the old center chimney and placing the fireplaces on the end walls.

Detail of Entrance and Pediment
APTHORP HOUSE—1760—CAMBRIDGE, MASSACHUSETTS

Before turning to the houses of square plan, let us look for a moment at the little house in Hingham—also of L-shape—locally known as the Bulfinch House. Local legend persists in claiming that it is formed from the upper two stories of an old house, once on Bowdoin, near Bulfinch Street, in Boston, of which the lower story had been of brick, which was taken down in 1841, and this upper part rafted down the harbor in parts on a packet, carried part way up the hill, and re-erected on its present site. The charming and unusual corner pilaster is,

the lower portion serving as the old shed, with five beautiful arches, some of which are now filled in.

The Apthorp House in Cambridge is an example of the more stately type of square Colonial house plan, of which the next two or three houses mentioned are further variants. These houses were oftentimes graced with roof balustrades, preferably along the upper roof deck. As the chimneys with this plan were normally placed on the outside wall, they also often had brick ends. It is, in New England, the local

Photograph by Wilfred A. French

DALTON HOUSE—BETWEEN 1750 AND 1760—NEWBURYPORT, MASSACHUSETTS

This picture is of special interest as showing the house before its recent restoration.

at any rate, excuse enough for including the house here! The sturdy simplicity of the doorway is also suggestive of Bulfinch's hands.

The house built by Commodore Joshua Loring in 1757 in old Roxbury is a rarely dignified and beautiful relic of a pre-Revolutionary mansion. The entrance was originally on the west side, where two beautiful Corinthian pilasters and capitals still show beneath a porch construction put on at this end a number of years ago. The present north doorway, opening on the garden, might, solely because of its greater refinement, also be suspected as a possible later addition. At the back is a separate building, designed for servants' rooms on the second floor,

representative of the Westover type that was equally representative of the South. When built for the occupancy of a colonial bishop in 1760, it did not include the third story now shown over the pediment in the photograph of the entrance, although it was added very soon afterward—according to one story, to serve as the slaves' quarters. While removed from its old site, and now surrounded by college dormitories, it still appears to dignified advantage, largely because of its foreground. It is interesting to note how superior this doorway is, in strength and decision of detail, to the similar treatment to be seen on the Longfellow House, built at practically the same time—

Photograph by courtesy of J. T. Kelley

TAYLOE HOUSE—1790—ROXBURY, MASSACHUSETTS

One of the best examples of a refined New England Colonial house in wood.
The porches and iron balconies, all old, are rather exceptional in treatment.

Photograph by Julian Buckly

HOUSE—c1800—WAYLAND, MASSACHUSETTS

This house is owned by Ralph Adams Cram, Architect, who added the balustrade to the main house and raised the roof of the old woodshed extension to obtain rooms in the second story.

GOVERNOR WILLIAM DUMMER HOUSE, BYFIELD, MASSACHUSETTS

An example of the prim New England type with fireplaces on the outer end walls.

EMERY HOUSE, NEWBURYPORT, MASSACHUSETTS

Built in 1796 by Thomas Coker, Architect. A good example of the New England gambrel roof type.

1759—and of precisely similar type, standing barely three quarters of a mile away on Brattle Street. Most beautiful and aristocratic of all the New England houses of this kind, however, was the old Tayloe House in Roxbury, near the Dorchester line. Its details were notable for their delicacy and refinement, while the house, though of a regular and consistently popular plan, yet possessed minor and unusual elements, including a rounding bay and two story porch at the rear.

An instance of a house with a lateral ell extension, although of later date, is an old house at Wayland, now owned by the architect, Mr. Ralph Adams Cram.

Detail of Entrance Vestibule
BENNETT HOUSE, WAYLAND, MASSACHUSETTS
This is a recent addition, as is generally the case where this feature is found.

There happen to be two fairly well known examples of old garden houses in New England: one the summer-house that, up to ten or a dozen years ago, stood back of the Royall House in Medford, on top of an artificial mound that, as a matter of fact, enclosed the old ice-house of the estate. While the summer-house has now nearly disappeared, one section of it still remains and has been preserved with the hope of sooner or later restoring it to its accustomed site. Along with this is shown the so-called tea-house belonging to the Elias Haskett Derby estate, on Andover Street at Peabody, supposed to have been built in 1799 by Samuel McIntire.

BENNETT HOUSE—c1800—WAYLAND, MASSACHUSETTS
Situated at the beginning of the Old Connecticut Path. This house, although late in date, is refined and delicate in treatment. The outside vestibule composes harmoniously with the rest of the design.

From the Halliday Collection, Boston

CRAIGIE-LONGFELLOW HOUSE, CAMBRIDGE, MASSACHUSETTS

Built in 1759 by Col. John Bassell.
While similar in general scheme to the Tayloe House, the detail is of a bolder
type. The doorway may also be compared with that of the Apthorp House.

Garden Front

LORING HOUSE, OLD ROXBURY, MASSACHUSETTS

Built in 1757 by Commodore Joshua Loring.
Commodore Loring was chief naval officer in command of the King's ships in the colonies.

Detail of Garden Doorway
COMMODORE LORING HOUSE, OLD ROXBURY, MASS.

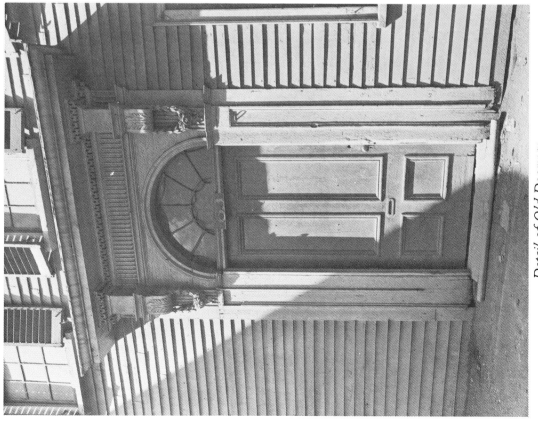

Detail of Old Doorway
HOUSE ON WASHINGTON STREET, BROOKLINE, MASS.

Photograph by Wilfred A. French

ROYALL SUMMERHOUSE AT MEDFORD, MASSACHUSETTS

Built in 1732. One section still remains.

Photograph by Frank Cousins

ELIAS H. DERBY TEA-HOUSE, PEABODY, MASSACHUSETTS

Supposed to have been built in 1799 and attributed to Samuel McIntire.

Early Brickwork in New England

Text by
Frank Chouteau Brown
Photographs by
Arthur C. Haskell
Originally published in 1934 as White Pine Monograph
Volume XX, Number 2

McPHEDRIS-WARNER HOUSE—1718-1723—PORTSMOUTH, NEW HAMPSHIRE

EARLY BRICKWORK IN NEW ENGLAND

ONE of the first references to brickmaking in New England occurs in "New England's Plantation; or a short and true Description of the Commodities and Discommodities of that county. Written in the year 1629 by Mr. Higgeson, a Reverend Divine, now there resident." In that year he writes of the "clay soyle—all about our plantation at Salem, for so our towne is now named, Psal 76.2." He continues, "It is thought here is a good clay to make bricke and tyles and earthen-pot as need to be. At this instant we are setting a brick-kill on worke to make brickes and tyles for the building of our houses."

On the 23rd of August, 1630, "at the First Court of Assistants holden at Charlton (Charlestown), it was ordered that carpenters, joyners, bricklayers, sawyers and thatchers shall not take aboue 2 s/ a day, nor any man shall giue more, under paine of 10 s/ to taker and guier." (This from the Records of the Colony of Massachusetts Bay in New England.) In Boston, in 1636, Thomas Mount was granted a piece of marsh "for the making of brick in," and "to Jaspar Rawlines," in 1644, was granted "use of a rood of upland for the making of Brickes." Of William Coddington's Boston house, which was probably patterned after some building in his own home town of Boston in Lancashire, he says, "Before Boston was named, I built the first good house," and of it Winsor writes, "Nor were there lacking mansions of more pretensions at the early time. When Coddington went from Boston to found his Colony of Rhode Island he had already built there a brick house, which, when

old, he still remembered as a token of his former magnificence."

An order issued on the 31st day of the 3rd month of 1658 by the General Court has especial interest in this connection; "Whereas Jno Conny was prohibited to burne brickes in his lott behind his house, and yett notwithstanding hath presumed to sett his kilne, Itt is ordered that in case he fire the kilne he shall pay ten shillings a day as a fine during the fire being in itt." In 1660 another order of the General Court is recorded, to give "Richard Gridley and ye rest of ye brickmakers in town . . . with what land may bee fitt for their use in ye most convenient place"—on Boston Common!

On May 28, 1679, an order of the General Court was enacted, in Boston, as follows:—"It is ordered by this Court & authority thereof, that clay to make bricks shall be digged before the 1st of November, & turned ouer in the moneth of February & March ensuing, a moneth before it is wrought, and that no person temper their bricks with salt water or brackish, and that the size of bricks be nine inches long, two & one quarter inches thicke & fower & a halfe inches broad, and that all moulds vsed for making bricke be made according to these sizes, and well shod with iron, & what person or persons soeuer shall make bricks in any respect contrary to this oeder, in the seuerall particulars of it, shall forfeite the one halfe of such bricks to the vse of the beauty of the toune where they are made." The law enacted in England in 1625, the first year of Charles I, established the

CHRIST CHURCH (OLD NORTH)—1723—SALEM STREET, BOSTON, MASSACHUSETTS

The bricks vary from 7¾″ to 8¼″ x 3⅝″ to 3⅞″ x 1¾″ to 1⅞″, laid English bond with joints about ⅜″ wide. 5 courses to 11 inches of height

OLD SOUTH MEETING HOUSE—1729—WASHINGTON STREET, BOSTON, MASSACHUSETTS

The bricks are 8″ x 3¾″ x 2″, laid Flemish bond with ⅜″ joint.

5 courses to 12 inches of height

Detail of Brick Bond
JOSEPH PEASLEE GARRISON — 1675 —
ROCK VILLAGE, MASSACHUSETTS

legal sizes of the English brick as 9″ x 4½″ x 3″.

Following after the "great fires" in Boston's early history, 1653, 1676, and 1679, it was ordered that no dwelling houses "except of stone and bricke, and couered with slate or tyle" be allowed to be built; an order which was modified in the following spring, establishing three years of grace, because of the poverty of those who had lost their property during the fire.

Most old architecture of the New England cities (where the houses were usually located — rather than in the country, as they were through the South) has suffered either through fire, or prosperity. Many brick buildings have survived the former, but fallen before the latter enemy, that has been the cause of the demolition of many an unusual and unique structure. The Old Brick Church, dedicated in Boston on May 3, 1713, for instance; a square structure, three stories high, with a two-story entrance vestibule; and the most costly house of worship built in this country up to that time, it was torn down in 1808.

Two of the earliest remaining church structures in Boston are Christ Church, better known perhaps as the Old North, and the Old South Meeting House. The Old North was built in 1723, 50 by 70 feet, and the spire of the tower, originally 191

feet tall, was blown down in 1804, and replaced, at a slightly smaller size, by Charles Bulfinch, to a height of 175 feet. Services are still maintained in Christ Church, as they have been, continuously, except through the brief period when interrupted by the occupancy of the British forces.

The Old South, built a few years after the Old North, in 1729, by one Joshua Blanchard, a Master Mason, who also built the first Faneuil Hall in 1742, is now kept open as a museum, though occasionally used for special meetings, to which its meeting house plan, with the pulpit high upon one long side and balconies around the other three, is especially adapted.

The Hall built by Peter Faneuil, originally in 1742, from plans by the painter John Smibert, at 40 by 100 feet and two stories high, was burned out in 1761, and rebuilt within the old walls by 1763, from the proceeds of a lottery authorized by the General Court. In 1805–1806 it was enlarged by Charles Bulfinch to its present size, 80 x 100 feet, and increased in height. The older part — that along the south side, from which the detailed photograph showing the windows is taken — extends up to the top of the entablature over the second-story windows, the wall above that point being of the 1805–1806 construction. The changed nature of

Detail of Brick Bond
OLD STATE HOUSE, BOSTON, MASSACHUSETTS

OLD STATE HOUSE—1713–1747—HEAD OF STATE STREET, BOSTON, MASSACHUSETTS
The bricks are 8⅛″ x 3¾″ x 2¼″ laid in English bond with ½″ joint.
5 courses in about 13½ inches of height

Detail of Brickwork
POWDER HOUSE, MARBLEHEAD, MASSACHUSETTS

the brickwork is most apparent upon the two ends; the later brick being smoother and lighter in color, and lacking the dark headers of the earlier walls. The sizes are also different.

The oldest Town House in Boston was of wood, built in 1657. It was burned in the fire of 1711, and was replaced by a building of brick, finished in 1713. The interior was again burned out in 1747, and its old walls were incorporated into the present Old State House at the head of State Street. Both the bricks and the joints are unusually rough in texture; the oldest joints being worn deep behind the brick face.

Medford, originally known as Mistick, was founded in 1630—or possibly 1629—by Matthew Craddock, elected first Governor of Massachusetts Bay Colony in London on May 13, 1629. He never left England, but two of the ships which sailed with the *Arbella* in 1630 belonged to Craddock—the *Ambrose* and the *Jewel*, and he may have sent them to Medford at the suggestion of Governor Winthrop, whose Ten Hills Plantation was there.

The early records of Medford have been lost, and so the earliest report concerned with local brickmaking dates only from 1660, when a conveyance of land in West Medford—south of Boston Avenue and between Arlington Street and the river—is described as being "adjoining to Thomas Eames clay lands." Bricks from this yard sold in 1750 for 10 shillings per thousand, and in 1760 at 15 shillings. By 1795, the price had risen to four dollars; while in 1777 Medford's other—and even more famous—product could be bought for 3s.6d the gallon! Bricks were made as late as the middle of the eighteenth century on the Brickyard Pasture, north of Dr. Tufts House.

Not only was Medford famous for its brick for many years (during the Revolution the selectmen petitioned for help from Boston and Charlestown because "the business of Medford, being largely that of brickmaking," it had been badly damaged by the blockade) but it had led many other towns in establishing the industry. Jeremiah Page, for instance, who started brickmaking in Danvers, was born in Medford in 1722 from whence he removed to what is still known as the Col. Jeremiah Page House in Danvers.

In Medford, where the pressure of later growth has not been so great, several quite early examples of brick dwellings have been preserved down to the present day. Of these the earliest and most important is probably the variously titled Craddock or Peter Tufts House, on Riverside Avenue, formerly Ship Street,

Detail of Brickwork
MASSACHUSETTS HALL, CAMBRIDGE, MASSACHUSETTS

FANEUIL HALL (1742) ENLARGED BY CHARLES BULFINCH — 1805–1806 — BOSTON, MASSACHUSETTS
Old bricks are 7⅛″ x 3⅜″ x 2″ laid Flemish bond with ⅜″ joint.
5 courses in 11¼ inches of height

South Side
FANEUIL HALL—1742—BOSTON, MASSACHUSETTS

once ascribed to 1634, but now believed to have been built in 1682. The bricks vary from 8 to 8¼ inches long, from 4 to 4½ inches wide, and from 2 to 3 inches thick, and are the same color as bricks afterward made in East Medford; so, although the material is often stated as "brought from England as ballast," it is far more probably of local make.

The house usually now known as the Garrison House, just back of Medford Square, was built by

was bought by Isaac Royall after John Usher's death in 1726, and was then a house of two-story height, about 45 by 18 feet, with a center door and end chimneys, the original walls still showing on the ends and west side.

The date usually given to the first house built upon this site by Lieutenant Governor Usher is 1690; and the lower front part of the end wall shown in the photograph probably dates from about that time; which

Photo. The Halliday Historic Co.

TUFTS-CRADDOCK HOUSE — 1668 — MEDFORD, MASSACHUSETTS

Major Jonathan Wade probably between 1683 and 1689. It was originally smaller than at present, and has been several times altered — a statement that is also true of the Craddock or Tufts House.

The old Royall House includes, as part of its present structure, a house that may have been built by Gov. Winthrop for his dwelling at his Ten Hills Farm. It appears on a plan made in 1697 and was probably erected ten years or so before that date. It

theory is substantiated by its being laid in English bond, the favorite method for early brickwork in New England. Following his purchase of the house, it was rebuilt in 1738, "after the model of a Nobleman's House in Antigua," where the Royalist, Col. Royall, had a summer plantation. It was enlarged to two rooms in depth and raised to three stories height, either in one or two operations. There is a record of Col. Royall having bought brick, in 1750,

Recent photograph showing alterations   *An old photograph in The Halliday Historic Collection*

JONATHAN WADE HOUSE — 1683–1689 — MEDFORD, MASSACHUSETTS

from "the Brickyard Pasture . . . north of Dr. Tufts House"; and it may have been that the house was increased in height to three stories, possibly with a lean-to or other type of extension at the rear; and later rebuilt to its present size — with the front away from the present street, which was originally the principal entrance to the house, that side fronting upon a stone-paved carriage court, enclosed by a fence with imposing posts and railing upon the side opposite the house, beyond which was the formal garden.

While other brick houses in Medford are old, they are all much later than those briefly described; many having been built by the Hall family of which three still remain, side by side, on Main Street; only a short distance from the Jonathan Wade residence — probably built between 1683 and 1689 — itself enlarged and rebuilt to its present size by another member of the Hall family, one Benjamin, about 1785.

It is this same Jonathan Wade House on Pasture Hill Lane in Medford that was supposed to have been the model for the large brick country house Sir Harry Frankland built in Hopkinton — to which he brought his Marblehead love, Agnes Surriage, after his return from Europe, where she had saved his life in the Lisbon earthquake.

One other nearby center of brick building must also be mentioned, Cambridge. While many of its churches and oldest houses were built of wood; with the exception of its first building, Harvard College had chosen brick for its oldest "Halls." Of these, Massachusetts, built from the proceeds of a state lottery in 1720, is among the earliest now standing; and of especial interest from its variety in the use of brick bond.

Below the moulded brick watertable, the courses are laid in English bond. Upon the two fronts of the building to north and south, a Flemish bond is used, while the east end, particularly, runs in English bond from the line of the lower-story window sills up to the belt at the level of the fourth floor, and above that line the gable is built of brick laid in three courses of stretchers with a course of headers, alternating, up to the chimneys. These treatments are shown in the measured drawing (page 146) which endeavors to combine the end with the front details of the structure. The bricks run about 7¾" to 8" x 3¾" to 3⅞" x 2" in size, and are laid about 5 courses to 11¾" in height. The moulded brick used in the watertable is laid, reversed, as part of the cornice.

Two of the oldest remaining examples come from the region north of Boston; one being the old house in Greenland, New Hampshire, that undoubtedly dates from an early period, so that the local claim to the date of 1638 may be correct. The brick of which it is built was burned only a short distance away. Locally known as a Garrison House, it was probably only so used because of the durable material of the walls.

The porch or vestibule on the old Spencer-Pierce-Little House at Newbury, dating from about 1645–1650, is of a very crude, roughly dimensioned brick, with many individual pieces either especially made, or else of unusual sizes, while others may have been split or ground down to use in the arches, or other ornamental parts of the composition. It is the gable and treatment of this entrance that — along with the steep pitch of the roof — does so much to suggest the English character of the whole structure.

ROYALL HOUSE — 1690-1738 — MEDFORD, MASSACHUSETTS

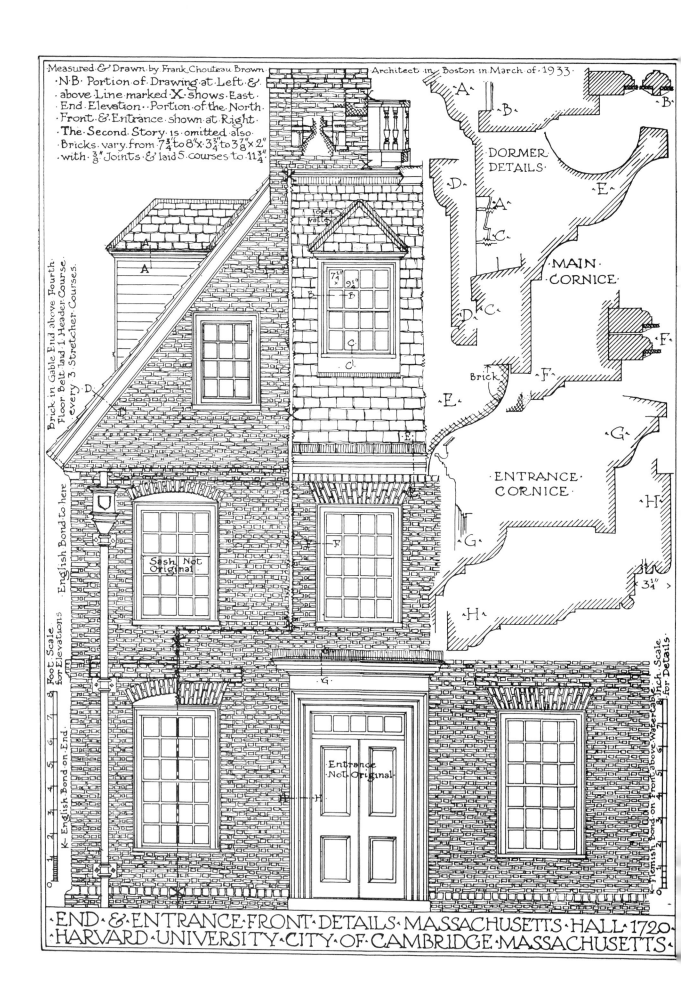

Measured & Drawn by Frank Chouteau Brown · Architect in Boston in March of 1933 ·
·N·B· Portion of Drawing at Left &
·above Line marked ·X· shows ·East·
·End· Elevation · Portion of the North·
·Front· & Entrance shown at Right·
·The Second Story is omitted also·
Bricks vary from 7¾ to 8 x 3¾ to 3⅞ x 2"
with ⅜" Joints & laid 5 courses to 11¾"

·A·
·B·

DORMER
DETAILS

·D·
·A·
·C·
·E·

MAIN·
CORNICE·

·D·C·
·F·

·E·
Brick
·F·

·G·

ENTRANCE·
CORNICE

·G·

·H·

3¼"

·H·

Brick in Gable End above Fourth
Floor Belt laid 1 Header Course
every 3 Stretcher Courses.

·D·

English Bond to here

·A·

7¼"
x
9¼"
·B·

·B·

·C·

·Cl·

Sash Not
Original

·F·

Foot Scale
for Elevations

K· English Bond on End

·G·

Entrance
Not Original

·H· ·H·

·X·

·ENTRANCE·WATER·CAP· Inch Scale
for Details

K Flemish Bond on Front above Water Cap.

·END· & ·ENTRANCE· FRONT· DETAILS· MASSACHUSETTS· HALL· 1720·
·HARVARD· UNIVERSITY· CITY· OF· CAMBRIDGE· MASSACHUSETTS·

MASSACHUSETTS HALL—1720—HARVARD UNIVERSITY, CAMBRIDGE, MASSACHUSETTS

The bricks vary from 7¾″ to 8″ x 3¾″ to 3⅞″ x 2″ with ⅜″ joints, laid 5 courses to 11¾ inches of height.

HOLLIS HALL—1763—HARVARD UNIVERSITY, CAMBRIDGE, MASSACHUSETTS
The bricks vary from 7¾" to 7⅞" x 3½" to 3⅝" x 2" to 2⅛" with ⅜" joints, laid in English bond.
5 full courses to 12½ inches of height

The Charm of
Old San Antonio

Text by
Harvery P. Smith
Photographs by
H. Patteson and H. L. Summerville
Originally published in 1931 as White Pine Monograph
Volume XVII, Number 4

THE ALAMO, SAN ANTONIO

Cradle of Texas Liberty

THE CHARM OF OLD SAN ANTONIO

FOR the student of early Spanish Colonial architecture in America, there are, perhaps, no finer examples to be found anywhere in the United States than the old missions and other historic buildings in and around San Antonio, Texas. There is a charm about these ancient edifices that quickens the imagination and leads you back into the romantic and picturesque days of the Spanish dons, the conquistadores, and the intrepid padres. These were the first pioneers who blazed the trails into the wilderness of the great southwest laying the foundation for the civilization which we now enjoy.

During the sixteenth, seventeenth, and the early part of the eighteenth centuries, Spain's desire for worldwide colonization included even the very remote parts of the newly discovered Americas. After Cortes wrested Mexico from the great Aztec chieftain, Montezuma, in 1521, that country became quickly settled with Spaniards until — during the seventeenth, and up to the beginning of the eighteenth century — Mexico itself, under Spanish rule, was sending out adventurers, missionaries, and colonists into the great unknown wilderness to the north.

Of the missionaries who went with these groups, the more famous are — Padre Junipero Serra, who established a line of missions along the coast of California, from San Diego to San Francisco; Father Kino, who established some missions in Arizona — the most famous of these being San Xavier del Bac, near Tucson; Fray Marcos, who established some of the early missions of New Mexico, and Father Antonio Margil, who came with an early group of Spanish soldiers and adventurers, traveling northeast into what is now Texas, establishing a line of garrisons and missions far into the interior — unconsciously reaching out toward the civilization extending westward from the New England colonies. The adventurers in these several expeditions were sent north by the Spanish Governors of Mexico, or under the direct order of the King of Spain, to search for gold. They had heard of the fabled "Seven Cities of Cibolo." Missionaries always accompanied these expeditions to give ecclesiastical sanction and approval to the adventure, but the avowed purpose of these self-sacrificing, devoted padres, was to Christianize the Indians, and to establish missions near all of the garrisons and colonies that were under the protection of the Crown.

One of these military expeditions sent out by the King of Spain, established a permanent garrison in 1718 on what is now Plaza de las Armas (or Military Plaza), in San Antonio. The missionaries, headed by Father Margil, who came with this expedition, so quickly developed their purpose in the community, that in 1720 — with only the aid of the Indian neophytes, and perhaps a very few skilled artisans of their own order — they began the construction of the first San Antonio mission, the justly-famous, San Jose de Aguayo, named after the Marquis San Miguel de Aguayo — one of the governors of Texas under the Spanish rule. From an architectural standpoint, it is undoubtedly the most beautiful and impressive of all the missions in the United States.

Though the construction was begun in 1720, it was not completed until March 5, 1731. Having taken eleven years to build, the day of its completion was celebrated by beginning the construction of three other missions near San Antonio, namely, La Purisima Concepcion de Acuna, San Francisco de la Espada, and the San Juan de Capistrano.

San Jose, however, is the only one of these missions, which lays any pretence to architectural design and detail. Pedro Huisar, the architect-sculptor, came over from Spain to go with the padres into this unknown region, leaving the impress of his genius in this lonely spot for future generations to enjoy. One of his ancestors carved much of the delicate tracery of the Alhambra, so Huisar, with his inherent ability, put his heart and soul into this one great work of his life and achieved some remarkable results.

The carving of the main façade is rich Renaissance — the doorway, however, has Moorish outlines. There are figures of virgins and saints, with realistic drapery, standing on pedestals, and recessed in niches with their conch-like canopies. Although the ornamentation is conventional, there is nothing stiff or wooden about it, every line and curve shows the freedom and mastery of the hand that carved it.

Exquisite as is the carving of this main entrance façade, it is even surpassed by the south window of the baptistry, which is considered the finest piece of Spanish Colonial ornamentation existing in America today. Its proportions and gracefully curving lines are an ever-present delight to the eye. The lover of sculptured detail never tires of looking at this window, as it is forever revealing some hidden beauty.

In addition to these, there are also several ornamental stone architraves, and, in the baptistry, pilaster caps, a baptisimal font, and other minor motifs.

Atop the lone tower is the beautifully proportioned belfry with its pyramidical stone roof. In the angle, formed by the tower and the wall of the nave, is a small, round tower, enclosing a circular stair—the steps built up, one upon the other, of solid hewn oak logs. In the east entrance to the baptistry—swinging on the same wrought iron hinges for two hundred years—are a pair of beautifully carved panel doors. Made of mesquite wood—found locally—the carved panels of these doors are exquisite, both in design and execution. Lintels of solid walnut have been found in this and the other missions.

The walls of the church are from three to five feet thick of solid limestone. One marvels at the engineering ability of these old padres in erecting the great, arched stone roof over the nave without the aid of modern machinery, and yet its construction was comparatively simple. As the outer walls were built up, dirt was filled in, and a long ramp of dirt built out in front, until the base of the arched roof was reached, when additional dirt was shaped up in a great curved mound. The roof stones were then set in place on this mound and locked with a keystone in the center. When the mortar had completely set, the earth was dug out from beneath, leaving the completed structure.

It is interesting to note the long cloister back of the church, the refectory, and the monk's cells, and in back of these, the old kitchen with its oven of handmade bricks, still fairly intact. Unfortunately, from an architectural standpoint, some Benedictine Fathers took over the old mission in 1859, with the intention of rehabilitating and occupying the building. Eager to rebuild according to their ideas, numerous Gothic arches were added—made with red bricks of their own manufacture—thus destroying, to some extent, the unity of the style established by Huisar.

Legends of buried treasure, started men digging about the walls, until on one stormy night of Decem-

ber 1868 the great dome and the roof over the nave fell with a crash. These were never rebuilt. Last year, the tower, which had been gradually weakening, under the continuous battle with the elements, fell to the ground, but this has been restored so well that only the practiced eye of a trained man could detect the restoration.

In the northwest corner of what was originally the quadrangle of the mission, there still stands today the old granary—unique because it is the only building of this type having flying stone buttresses, and because it was built and used prior to the church building itself.

San Francisco de la Espada is the only one of the missions, which still possesses, to a marked degree, the original atmosphere and completeness of the quadrangle, as it was first built. This mission lies off the beaten trail on a winding road over which the padres must have trudged many a time in their travels from mission to mission. The little church is very simple—its only distinguishing features being the Moorish doorway and the campanile with its mission bells. Either the ruined walls, or the entire structure, of each building that formed the outer walls of the quadrangle can still be seen, almost as it was then. On the outer, southeast corner,

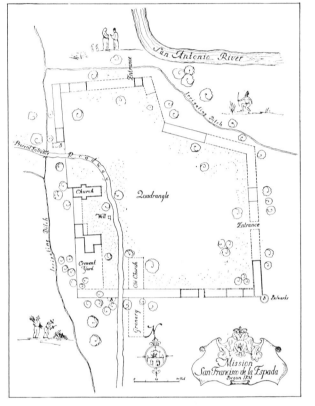

PLAN OF QUADRANGLE

still stands a sturdy, little, circular stone fort. Whenever the mission was besieged by the Indians, all the inhabitants, who lived in and around the walls, would hurry inside and barricade themselves—the men fighting from the little fort. The rifle holes are hardly larger than a silver dollar on the outside, widening to a diameter of two to three feet at the inner surface of the wall. Two holes for small cannon are still to be seen.

Mission San Juan de Capistrano is the one of this group farthest south from San Antonio, although none of them are very far from the heart of the city, being approximately two miles apart along the El Camino Real (the King's Highway). Capistrano is, perhaps,

Plan of Quadrangle on Opposite Page
MISSION SAN FRANCISCO DE ESPADA, STARTED 1731

Entrance Detail

THE ALAMO, SAN ANTONIO, TEXAS

the least interesting of all the missions here, and yet, the walls of practically all the buildings surrounding the quadrangle are still visible, though many a load of stone has been hauled off to build some little farm building nearby.

Still another mission, and probably the most famous of all the missions in and about San Antonio, is San Antonio de Valero (built in 1744) and everywhere known and spoken of as the Alamo (Spanish for cottonwood — there being a grove of cottonwoods nearby). The reason for its fame being neither its architecture, which is simple, nor its success as a mission, which was negligible, but rather because of the fact that it was the "Cradle of Texas Liberty." Here in 1836 took place a battle, the like of which has never been surpassed, and seldom equaled, anywhere else in the world. It was the result of this battle, in which every man of the 177 pioneer Texans lost their lives, that caused the overthrow of Mexican domination and the establishment of Texas as an independent republic. The façade is the only point of architectural interest. Its very simplicity being the chief attraction.

While there are, perhaps, fifty or more missions left in the United States, San Antonio boasts the unique distinction of being the only city which possesses more than one (and it has five!) — all in a fairly good state of preservation.

Beside the missions, there is an old Governors' Palace, which has stood on Military Plaza for nearly two hundred years, and was just recently restored. The carved keystone over the main entrance states that it was built in the "Año 1749." Architecturally, it could not be rated very high, but the charm of the crude little one-story building, and the fidelity with which the restoration preserved and brought back to life the original atmosphere of this residence of the early Spanish Governors is unmistakable. You can easily imagine (as at Mount Vernon) that most any minute the original master of the house will step out of the door.

In addition to this, there are numerous old stone houses, a wonderful aqueduct, built by the padres, with water flowing over it still, after 200 years of continuous service, also many minor structures of historic and picturesque interest.

It seems a shame to think of the numerous old buildings and homes, which have been torn down to make room for little, one-story, unimportant, modern structures, and sometimes just a parking lot, when there are acres and acres of ugly, uninteresting buildings, which could be removed — with resulting satisfaction for most of us — to make room for modern progress, and save the few gems of Spanish Colonial architecture remaining in our midst. But these heritages from the past are gradually coming into their own. The consciousness of the people, through the efforts of a few devoted architects, artists, and lovers of the romantic and the picturesque, has been aroused to the necessity of preserving, and, where possible, restoring to their pristine glory, these grand old monuments of another day.

Rendering of the Patio by Harvey P. Smith
OLD SPANISH GOVERNOR'S PALACE, SAN ANTONIO, TEXAS

Main Façade
MISSION SAN JOSE DE AGUAYO, NEAR SAN ANTONIO

Interior of Doorway from Baptistry
MISSION SAN JOSE DE AGUAYO, NEAR SAN ANTONIO

Interior of Baptistry

MISSION SAN JOSE DE AGUAYO, NEAR SAN ANTONIO

Baptismal Font, Baptistry

Capital in Baptistry

MISSION SAN JOSE DE AGUAYO, NEAR SAN ANTONIO

Entrance to Baptistry
MISSION SAN JOSE DE AGUAYO, NEAR SAN ANTONIO

Harvey P. Smith, Architect for the Restoration

Doorway With Keystone of Hapsburg Coat-of-Arms
OLD SPANISH GOVERNOR'S PALACE, SAN ANTONIO

MISSION SAN JOSE DE AGUAYO, NEAR SAN ANTONIO

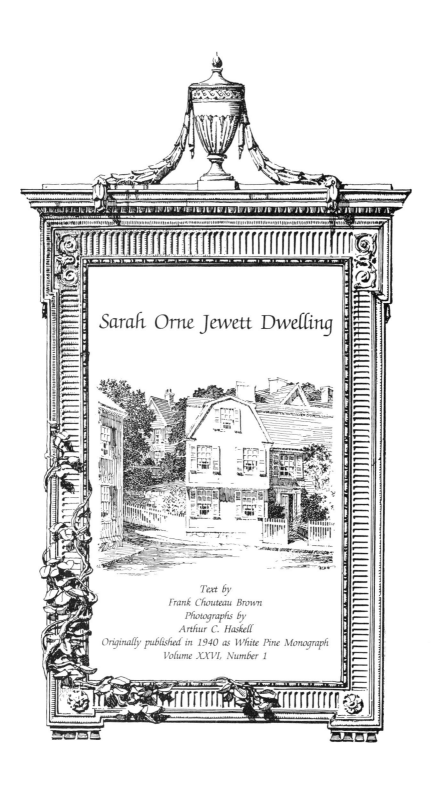

Sarah Orne Jewett Dwelling

Text by
Frank Chouteau Brown
Photographs by
Arthur C. Haskell
Originally published in 1940 as White Pine Monograph
Volume XXVI, Number 1

Detail View of South Entrance Front
SARAH ORNE JEWETT HOUSE — 1774 — SOUTH BERWICK, MAINE

THE INTERIOR DETAILS AND FURNISHINGS OF THE SARAH ORNE JEWETT DWELLING BUILT BY JOHN HAGGINS IN 1774, AT SOUTH BERWICK, MAINE

AMONG the areas "set apart" from the older township of Kittery in 1713 is the land that was again subdivided, a century later, in 1814, into Berwick, North Berwick (where the railroad station now is) and South Berwick—which is the present name of what was the old village or original town settlement upon the Maine side of the river from Salmon Falls, now in New Hampshire. In this Kittery section, as in so many other parts of the region round about, the architecture stems from the old Portsmouth types, and the more important houses were probably built by the same builders who had "raised" the better places in Portsmouth—located at the mouth of the Piscataqua, and the "port" of the inland region back of it along Great Bay and the navigable stretches of the confluent rivers.

Some of the other old dwellings—and most of those earlier than the Jewett Mansion—have disappeared during the last twenty or thirty years, fortunately leaving this structure, which from the records kept by one Master Taite in an old journal, we know was built by John Haggins or Higgins. He wrote, "Mr. John Higgins raised a new house at the turn of the ways near Mr. Robert Rodgers on Berwick side on Thursday, April ye 7th, 1744." When Hamilton House was built a year later—lower down on the same side of the river, with its own wharf and warehouses—it was directed to be "larger than John Haggins' house." Hamilton House is the single other fine mansion remaining in this part of the township, to maintain the Portsmouth tradition; the Judge Haynes House, set high upon its steep-rising hillside on the road to York, being of a later and quite different type. Of the builder, John Haggins or Higgins, little has been discovered, except that it is known he loved convivial company, his pipe and his toddy, and probably spent many a night at the town inn, from which, tradition says, his wife Nancy had often to drag him, when the nine o'clock bell rang! Years later, the property passed into the hands of Captain Theodore Jewett, whose son, Dr. Jewett, was well patronized in the countryside, judging by the eight granite hitching posts and horse block that remain today. He was the father of Mary and Sarah Orne Jewett.

The house is large and square, with the end roof slopes far steeper than those to front and back—a Portsmouth peculiarity that also marked the roof of another old house, formerly across the square nearby, but long since disappeared, and several old Portsmouth dwellings, including the Tobias Lear House (c1740), still standing just around the corner from the Wentworth-Gardner House (1760). The Jewett House, as it has now come to be known, is set rather near the street, with a gate (of somewhat older design than the present fence) opening upon the brick walk to the front door. The door is protected by an unusual pedimented porch, which is in turn overhung by old, crowding lilac shrubs, bordered by dwarf box.

The house fronts the village square (actually a triangle), with the town blacksmith shop (now a garage) and post office, across the way. Older pictures (page 167) show the house with what appears to be a balustraded "walk" along the roof ridge, but this was rather an ornamental roof cresting, of considerably later date. The original corner trim appears to have been quoins, later replaced by the more conventional corner-boards (page 168). Although the kitchen in the rear ell is apparently as old as the main house, the second-story finish of the servants' rooms, and bath that it now contains, is all more recent. The old-fashioned privy and laundry are at the extreme north end of the ell, along with a capacious side entry and storeroom.

NOTE: *This mansion is owned and maintained by The Society for the Preservation of New England Antiquities, and is now being measured as a Maine Record by the Historic American Buildings Survey.*

But it is in the main part of the house that the most architectural and sentimental interest remains. The entrance hall is unusually beautiful (see page 175, and also Volume X, Chapter 10) with many of the best details of the Portsmouth tradition gathered in this one example. The same finish is carried up into the second hall, which reminds one particularly of the same space in the Wentworth-Gardner House, although lacking the large plaster cove. The heavy cornice, door cap and entablature have caused the doors—particularly upon the second floor—to be kept very low; and both the first hall archway, and the arched window top on the staircase landing (see Volume X, Chapter 9), have an unusually shaped and carved "key" ornament. The staircase has other unusual features, along with the "reversed bracket run," used as a skirtboard along the stair dado, as elsewhere in Portsmouth dwellings of the same or earlier period. The local legend is that the finish of the stairs and the two halls took two men one hundred days of labor to complete ("long" days, not the "union labor" hours of today!). The woodwork in

the hall, and in some other parts of the house, remained unpainted until 1838, when it had ripened to a beautiful tobacco brown tone.

The first floor room at the right, once Mary Jewett's library, but now a parlor furnished simply in the period of the rest of the house, contains an original fireplace treatment, without mantel shelf or the earlier bolection moulding. Across the hall, on the southwest corner of the house, is the more elaborately detailed parlor, a beautiful room, with the cornerposts converted into fluted pilasters after the Portsmouth fashion. A mantel, probably later in date, but finely worked by carpenter's chisel-carving, is notable in this room; and in the passage beside the fireplace connecting it with the dining room, are two simple, (and also later) glass cupboards, with glazed doors for the "best chiney." Here the finish and detail are much simpler. By crossing the hall back of the staircase into the breakfast room, a still earlier and sterner treatment—in accord with the old kitchen beyond—will be found. At the east of the chimney on this side of the house is the usual "secret staircase" that runs

General View From Southwest
SARAH ORNE JEWETT HOUSE—1774—SOUTH BERWICK, MAINE

General View of House From Southeast
This view, taken in 1935, shows upper roof balustrade in position.

General View of House From Northwest
SARAH ORNE JEWETT HOUSE — 1774 — SOUTH BERWICK, MAINE

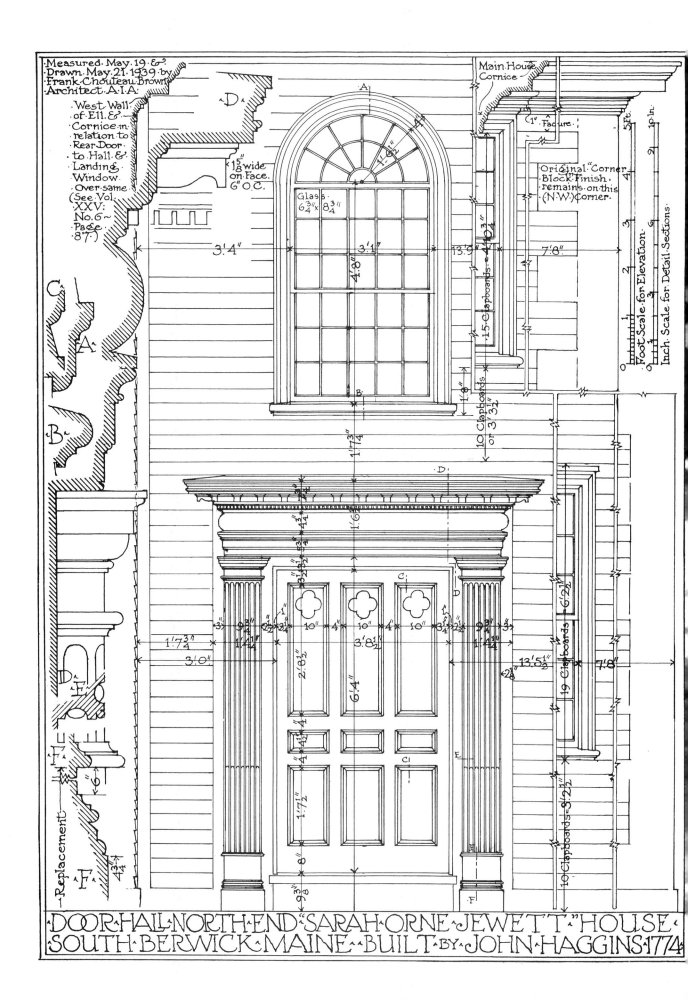

Measured May 19 &
Drawn May 21 1939 by
Frank Chouteau Brown
Architect A.I.A.

West Wall
of Ell &
Cornice in
relation to
Rear Door
to Hall &
Landing
Window
Over same
(See Vol.
XXV.
No. 6 ~
Page
87.)

·D·

1⅝ wide
on Face.
6" O.C.

·C·
·A·
·B·

Glass
6¾" x 8¾"

·A·

3'4"

3'1"

4'8"

·B·

13'9"

15 Clapboards = 4'0¾"

7'8"

1'8"

10 Clapboards
or 3'3 9/32"

1'7¾"

·D·

1'6⅝"

3'8½"

·C·

10" 4" 10" 4" 10" 3¾"

1'7¾"

3'0"

2'8½"

6'4"

·D·

13'5½"

2⅝"

19 Clapboards = 6'2½"

7'8"

·C₁·

1'7½"

·E·

8"

9¾"

·F·

10 Clapboards = 3'2½"

Main House
Cornice

1" Facure

Original "Corner
Block" Finish
remains on this
(N.W.) Corner.

5 Ft
4
3
2
1
0

Foot Scale for Elevation

10 In
9
8
7
6
5
4
3
2
1
0

Inch Scale for Detail Sections

Replacement
·F·

·D·
·E·

·F·
6"

4¾"

·DOOR·HALL·NORTH·END·"SARAH·ORNE·JEWETT"·HOUSE·
·SOUTH·BERWICK·MAINE·~·BUILT·BY·JOHN·HAGGINS·1774·

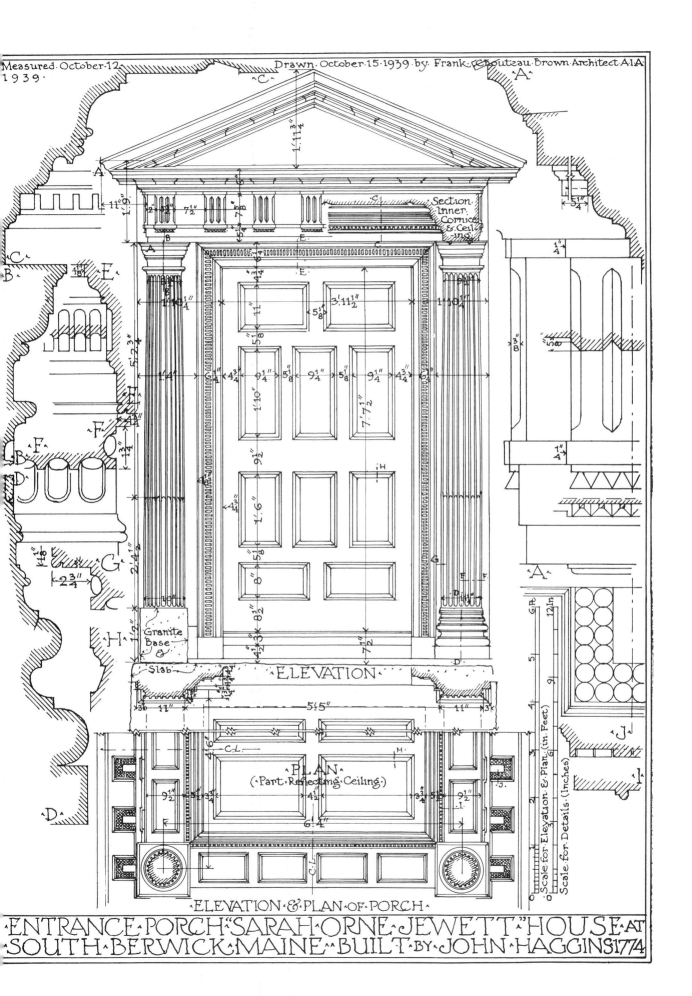

Measured. October. 12.
1939.

Drawn. October. 15. 1939. by. Frank. Chouteau. Brown. Architect. A.I.A.

Section.
Inner.
Cornice.
& Ceiling.

·ELEVATION·

Granite
Base
&
Slab

·PLAN·
(·Part·Reflecting·Ceiling·)

Scale for Elevation. & Plan. (in Feet.)

Scale. for Details. (Inches.)

·ELEVATION· & ·PLAN· OF· PORCH·

·ENTRANCE·PORCH·"SARAH·ORNE·JEWETT"·HOUSE·AT·
SOUTH·BERWICK·MAINE··BUILT·BY·JOHN·HAGGINS·1774·

North Entrance Doorway

South Entrance Porch

SARAH ORNE JEWETT HOUSE — 1774 — SOUTH BERWICK, MAINE

Southeast Bedroom Doorway, Looking into Hall

Hall Doorway, Looking into Southwest Parlor

SARAH ORNE JEWETT HOUSE—1774—SOUTH BERWICK, MAINE

West End of Parlor (Southwest Room), First Floor

Southeast Room, First Floor, Formerly Mary Jewett's Library
SARAH ORNE JEWETT HOUSE—1774—SOUTH BERWICK, MAINE

Northwest (Family Dining) Room, First Floor

Northeast (Family Breakfast) Room, First Floor
SARAH ORNE JEWETT HOUSE – 1774 – SOUTH BERWICK, MAINE

from here to the attic floor two stories above. It is actually only the "side stairs" of colonial tradition, but in this house lacks any outside doorway to the east. The old dresser in the kitchen was formerly fitted with old blue Chinese willowware.

On the second floor the stair rail is very high — appearing the more so from the low ceiling appearance due to the heavy hall cornice — but is gracefully curved in plan as well as ramped in elevation, at both the landing and end of the stairwell. This effect also partially duplicates that in the Wentworth-Gardner House. The two black horsehair sofas,

Detail of Front Porch Column and Cornice

described in Laura E. Richards recollections of the house, still stand on either side at the front of the second hall.

On this floor four bedrooms occupy the same locations as the rooms below, that in the southwest corner being again the most elaborate. Once more cornerposts, mantelpiece, dado, cornice, and door and window trim are fondly elaborated — chisel-cut and hand-molded by carpenter's tools. This room belonged to Mary, and the one across the hall, on the southeast corner, with its simpler finish, was the guest room. Going through the passage beside the hidden stair, one comes to

Old Kitchen and Fireplace in North Ell
SARAH ORNE JEWETT HOUSE — 1774 — SOUTH BERWICK, MAINE

Main Hall and Stairway, Looking toward Front Door
SARAH ORNE JEWETT HOUSE — 1774 — SOUTH BERWICK, MAINE

Sarah's room, which still contains its old Victorian furniture and arrangement, just as it was left by Sarah Jewett, even to the heavy green color of the paint! The room in the northwest corner, over the dining room, belonged to Theodore, the nephew, Dr. Eastman, while north of Sarah's room opened the bath, and beyond that was the servants' ell. The front door is large and unusually paneled, with huge wrought hinges, brass handle and knocker.

The attic was finished about 1870, to which period also belong the overlarge and aggressive dormers.

"Secret Stairway" Between the East Rooms, Looking from Breakfast Room

Many wall papers and curtains remain to display their Victorian traditions, even those (page 172) spread out over the floor below the windows! The southwest bedroom still has a beautiful old maroon flock paper, patterned in worn white and silver mica. This paper was printed in 18 x 22 inch sections for a French Governor-General in the West Indies, but intercepted by a privateer and brought into Salem, where Capt. Jewett secured it. The other papers, while not as old, are in character with the house, its history, and the Victorian furniture of its famous occupants!

West Side of Second Story Hallway
SARAH ORNE JEWETT HOUSE—1774—SOUTH BERWICK, MAINE

Southeast Corner (Guest) Bedroom

Southwest Corner (Mary Jewett's) Bedroom
SARAH ORNE JEWETT HOUSE—1774—SOUTH BERWICK, MAINE

Mantel in Southwest (Mary's) Bedroom

SARAH ORNE JEWETT HOUSE—1774—SOUTH BERWICK, MAINE

Northwest (Dr. Theodore's) Bedroom

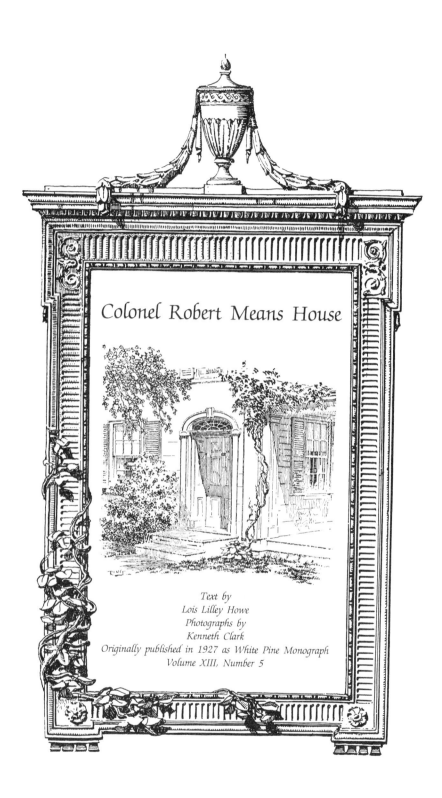

Colonel Robert Means House

Text by
Lois Lilley Howe
Photographs by
Kenneth Clark
Originally published in 1927 as White Pine Monograph
Volume XIII, Number 5

COLONEL ROBERT MEANS HOUSE, AMHERST, NEW HAMPSHIRE

THE COLONEL ROBERT MEANS HOUSE
AMHERST, NEW HAMPSHIRE

A DISTINGUISHED American authority on Gothic architecture is said to have made the statement that "there is no such thing as a village in America," the proof of which may be referred either to the point of view of a traveler or to his definition of a village.

If he looks for a picturesque huddle of houses with quaint broken lines and interesting textures of masonry and roof such as delights our eyes in Europe the statement is correct.

If, on the contrary, he consults a dictionary he will find the following definition, "village — a small assemblage of houses, less than a town or city and larger than a hamlet." With this idea in mind anyone who has traveled in this country will find here and there in the older states and particularly in New England a few such "assemblages" as yet unspoiled and with picturesque qualities of their own.

Such a village is Amherst, New Hampshire, not exactly off the beaten track, for a tarred and numbered road runs through it and so do automobiles with license plates of remote states. There are electric lights and the general store and garage have gasoline for sale; but the woodbine twining around the electric light poles seems to give a symbolic suggestion of its real aloofness from the world.

The location of the town has a good deal to do with this and goes to prove that environment is stronger than heredity. Originally, it was the shiretown of Hillsborough County as its disused court house shows, but now business has slipped away to the valley of the Merrimack, which flows seven miles to the east turning the wheels of many mills, and has carried the courts with it.

To the south, the railroad follows the valley of the Souhegan winding among the foothills of the Temple Mountains — that beautiful range which veils Monadnock from the Merrimack and tempts summer visitors to regions of wilder and more extended views than from Amherst Plain as the Common is called.

The village, however, has the advantage of its defects. The trolley car has avoided it and it has not a tearoom — a gift shop — nor a hot dog stand. Since the abandonment of the branch railroad which once came discreetly to its outskirts, the would-be tourist who has no motor must take a "bus" which leaves him three miles from the center.

Hence it is that it has kept its charm, a bit of Cranford in New England looking almost as it did in the days when it was a social and legal center.

It must be a full quarter of a mile from the Spaulding House at the west end of the Plain to the brick court house which faces it at the other end with the old graveyard behind it. And on either side besides the church, the public library, and the two stores are houses, each in its own large yard. Most of them are white with green blinds, some of them unimportant but there is not a "French roof" among them. And the Plain and the houses on it and on the side streets which radiate from it are overhung with beautiful trees culminating in a solemn group of pines in the graveyard.

Near the court house and the graveyard and cut off from the main road by a stretch of greensward bearing a magnificent elm stands the house which Colonel Robert Means built in 1785 (Monday, May 30, was the "raising").

Robert Means was born in Ireland in 1742. He was a weaver by trade and came to Boston with a friend in 1766. They first settled in Merrimack, carrying their wares about the country in their packs. It is astounding to find that their business increased so that they decided to establish another trade center at Amherst. Neither wanting to go, they tossed up for it and so Robert Means came to Amherst about 1774 bringing his young wife with him and here he lived until his death in 1823. At first he carried on his trade of weaving but later devoted himself to the mercantile side of the business keeping a sort of general store next to the house. By integrity and ability he amassed what was a large fortune for those times and had a position of high social as well as financial standing. He was a member of the legislature and held various offices, among them that of colonel of militia.

A year before Colonel Robert Means came to Amherst came Joshua Atherton, a lawyer and graduate of Harvard College with his wife and child. Between these men a life-long friendship sprang up. Their families intermarried and have been closely connected for over one hundred years.

After the Colonel's death his widow seems to have either sold or rented the house and for some twenty years it was occupied by outsiders. Robert Means, Jr., who had married Abigail Kent, the grandchild of Joshua Atherton, died in 1842 in Lowell where he had been superintendent of the Suffolk Mills. There were no children and his widow returned to Amherst and bought the old house. In it she established her mother and her brother George Kent and his wife.

It was her mother, Mrs. Amos Kent, who installed upon the staircase landing the busts of two of her brothers-in-law, their heads at the proper heights from the floor—the Honorable Jeremiah Mason, six feet seven inches tall, the Honorable Amos Lawrence, above five feet four inches tall.

She died in 1846 but George Kent and his wife lived there until his death in 1883 and there their only child Anna Kent was born. Mrs. Robert Means, Jr., left the house to her sister, Mrs. James MacGregor, to go after her death to Anna Kent now Mrs. Charles Theodore Carruth and to her son after her.

Wholly without pretense, the house stands with quiet dignity under the locust trees behind the white fence which gives it an old-fashioned privacy disdained by many modern communities.

It is a four square house with two chimneys, an ell with shed and barn parallel to the street giving it a long pleasing line. It is a very good New England example of the second period of Colonial architecture—the windows in pairs on either side of the front door, the latter hospitably wide, three panels wide, with fluted pilasters and a pediment with consoles.

In the center of each of the three other sides of the house is a similar doorway, that on the east being frankly an architectural decoration.

The hip roof, a little steeper than is usually found in this type is unbroken save at the south end where two dormers light the third story. This roof originally had a railing just above the dormers as is shown by an old engraving in the possession of the present owner.

The main cornice which has both consoles and dentils breaks around the second story window frames, the consoles being a little more closely spaced across them.

As if to justify this, there is a half console placed in profile against the fascia on each side of each window.

The interior is of charming proportions, distinctly domestic—the hall and staircase unusually beautiful, the latter recalling in its easy rise and tread that of the Lee Mansion in Marblehead though there is nothing grandiose about it. The balusters are turned and there are sawed stair ends. Beneath the stairs above the landing is a large panel with carved rosettes in the corners and below this there is a delightful vista through the wide garden door. The back staircase in the little hall between the two south rooms is also suggestive of the back staircase in the Lee Mansion and runs up two flights giving access to the "attic."

There is but one room in the main house which has not some interesting paneling. Six of them have paneled chimney breasts and some of them wainscot like that in the hall with chair rails at the level of the window stools. In two of the bedrooms the over-mantel is inset an inch between the end pieces instead of projecting.

To the parlor, of course, was given the greatest consideration. Here we have the pilaster treatment, the cornice breaking around the capitals as it also does around the window heads. But where have we before met a moulding like that around the fireplace—a small bolection moulding with ears and one carved member? And how exquisitely has Colonel Means suggested the solution of the problem of a mantel shelf with such a composition of fireplace and panel! The top member is, of course, a modern addition probably made by Abby Atherton Means.

As frequently happens in houses of this period, the windows in this, the best room, are recessed with seats and paneled shutters, the walls being thickened to get this effect which seems to have been purely decorative. Shutters which occur on every window on the ground floor, being probably intended for protection at night, are applied to some of the windows so as to swing clear into the room. In the sitting room they slide into pockets in the wall and are fastened with brass pegs kept hanging by the sides of the windows. The paneled recess and seat, but without shutters, is found again on the landing of the stairs where there is a well proportioned arched window.

It is worthy of note that while the front and rear doors and the windows over them are centered on the house, they are not centered on the hall. This is because the sitting room on the right of the hall is larger than the parlor on the left. The result is that from the entrance door there is a good view of the window on the landing.

COLONEL ROBERT MEANS HOUSE, AMHERST, NEW HAMPSHIRE

South Front
COLONEL ROBERT MEANS HOUSE, AMHERST, NEW HAMPSHIRE

The fourth room on the ground floor now used as a dining room was the original kitchen. It is sheathed with wide pine boards, somewhat after the fashion of the first period; these have never been painted. There Mrs. Abigail Atherton Kent Means did one dastardly deed. She took out the brick oven on the right-hand side of the fireplace. Cooking stoves had come in — why take up so much room with an obsolete oven when the space it occupied gave such a useful closet with a slide through to the closet in the dining room? The enormous hearth is still there to show where it stood. Let us be grateful to her that least she replaced it with a six-paneled door like the others in the room. We certainly owe her a debt of gratitude for moving away Colonel Means' shop which was a large two-story building, both shop and warehouse, which stood close to the south side of the house at the front.

But it was no part of Colonel Means' plan to have a joyless, cheerless house. He was famed for his hospitality and to Amherst in its prime came many lawyers when court was in session who were glad to find relaxation in the intervals of their professional duties in the society of the gay little town. Dances and card parties were frequent, the old letters tell us. So in the second story the wall between the hall and the bedroom, over the large sitting room, is handsomely paneled and hinged at the top so that it may be hooked up to make a ballroom. This arrangement was a simple proposition in a house framed after the fashion of the eighteenth century with self-supporting floors on which owners erected partitions where they chose.

Such is the Means House architecturally. It has, however, an unusual quality, an atmosphere, from the fact that for nearly eighty years it has been lived in by one family. It has been kept up but there has been a minimum of change or "restoration" and no dilapidation.

What Robert Means' furniture was like, we do not know. It went out with his wife and was probably scattered among his children. Some of it may have come back with his daughter-in-law. The house is as it was furnished in 1846. A purist, therefore, would wish to have many things "done over" as many of the furnishings especially the carpets are Victorian. Anyone who demands period furniture will be disappointed.

The fact is, however, that the mellowness and quaintness of the furnishings give the house more expression than if it were absolutely true to form. It seems full of the gentle lives that have been lived there.

The "modern conveniences"—plumbing, electric lights, heating, etc., have been added with affectionate care and effort not to spoil the effect and so have the up-to-date ornaments and accessories of furniture. They have all been introduced with an almost Ruskin-like feeling of necessity and have taken their places in the house as has the moss on the trees about it or the little ferns in the cracks of the bricks in the front walk, as part of the bloom of the whole.

Especially must be mentioned the wall papers in the hall and parlor, of date unknown, faded and stained, and yet so unusual and attractive that it would seem a sacrilege to change them.

And as we look at all the refinements of the finish even at some of its naiveties and crudities, we wonder where and how the weaver who peddled his goods about the country learned how to choose his proportions and details so wisely.

East Elevation
COLONEL ROBERT MEANS HOUSE, AMHERST, NEW HAMPSHIRE

Hall and Stairway

COLONEL ROBERT MEANS HOUSE, AMHERST, NEW HAMPSHIRE

East Wall of the Parlor, Northwest Room, First Floor

COLONEL ROBERT MEANS HOUSE, AMHERST, NEW HAMPSHIRE

Northeast Room, First Floor
COLONEL ROBERT MEANS HOUSE, AMHERST, NEW HAMPSHIRE

Detail of Gate and Entrance
COLONEL ROBERT MEANS HOUSE, AMHERST, NEW HAMPSHIRE

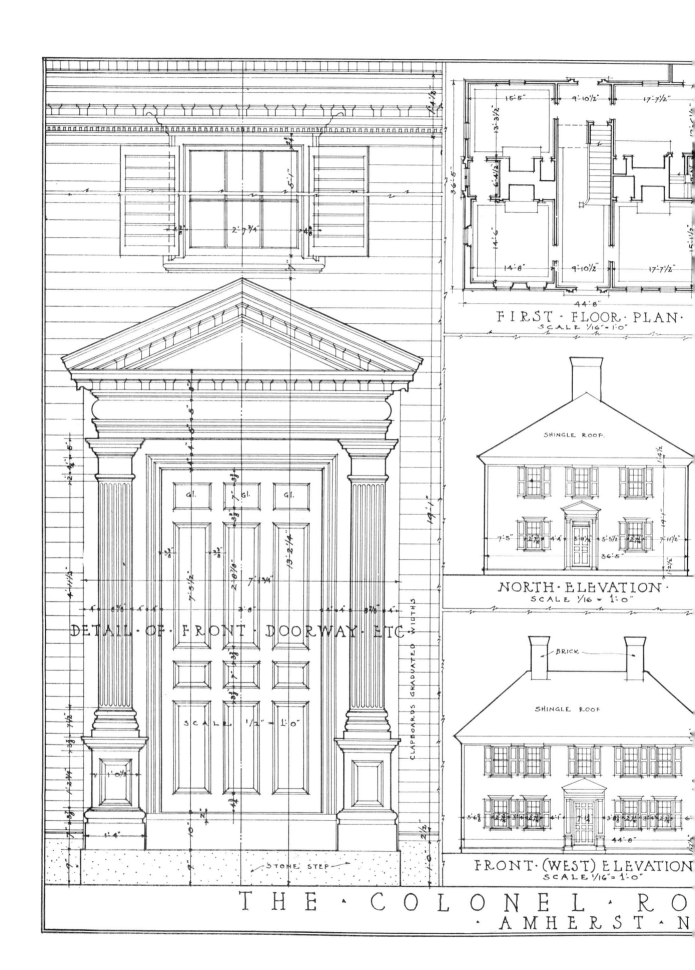

DETAIL·OF·FRONT·DOORWAY·ETC

SCALE 1/2" = 1'·0"

STONE STEP

FIRST·FLOOR·PLAN·
SCALE 1/16" = 1'·0"

NORTH·ELEVATION·
SCALE 1/16" = 1'·0"

SHINGLE ROOF.

SHINGLE ROOF

BRICK

FRONT·(WEST)·ELEVATION
SCALE 1/16" = 1'·0"

THE·COLONEL·RO
·AMHERST·N

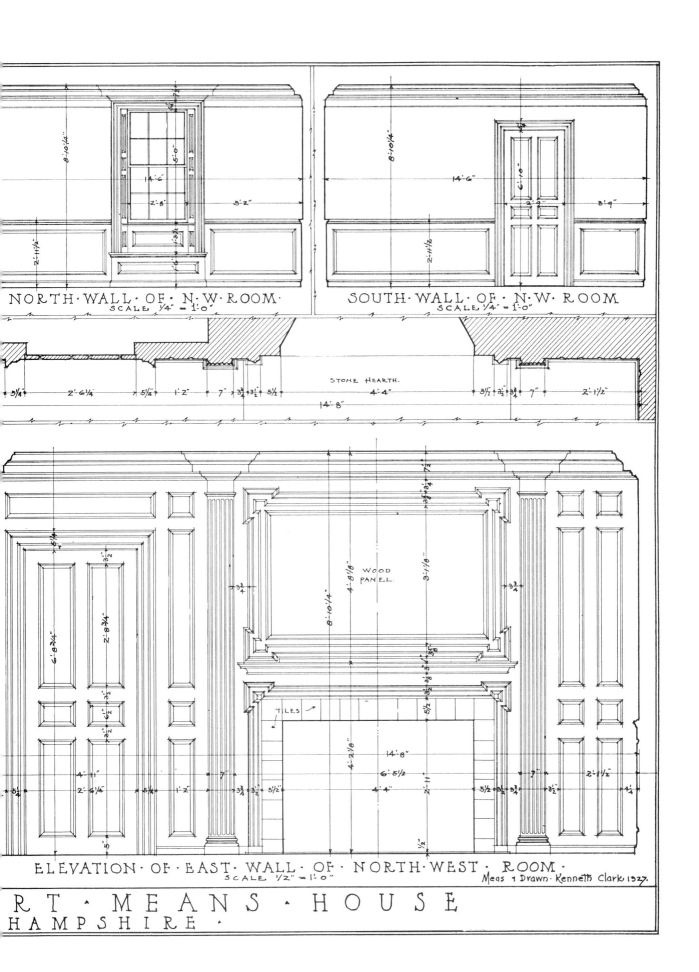

NORTH · WALL · OF · N.W. ROOM ·
SCALE 1/4" = 1'-0"

SOUTH · WALL · OF · N.W. ROOM
SCALE 1/4" = 1'-0"

STONE HEARTH.

WOOD PANEL.

TILES

ELEVATION · OF · EAST · WALL · OF · NORTH · WEST · ROOM ·
SCALE 1/2" = 1'-0"

Meas 1 Drawn · Kenneth Clark 1927.

RT · MEANS · HOUSE
HAMPSHIRE ·

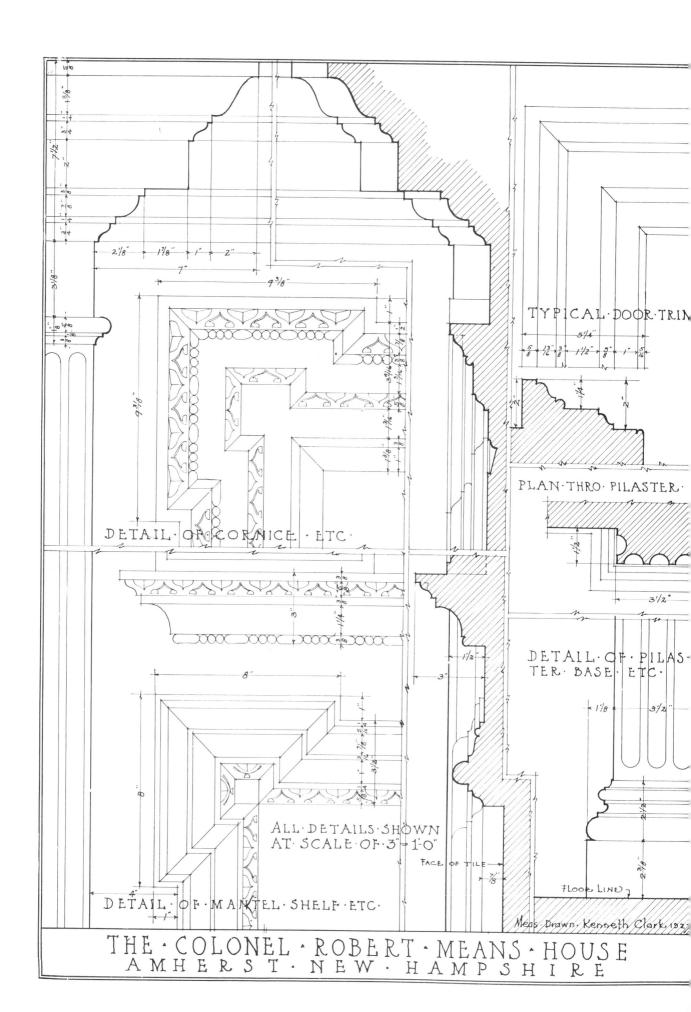

TYPICAL·DOOR·TRIM

PLAN·THRO·PILASTER·

DETAIL·OF·CORNICE·ETC·

DETAIL·OF·PILAS-
TER·BASE·ETC·

ALL·DETAILS·SHOWN
AT·SCALE·OF·3"=1'0"

FACE·OF·TILE

FLOOR·LINE

DETAIL·OF·MANTEL·SHELF·ETC·

Meas·Drawn·Kenneth·Clark·192

THE·COLONEL·ROBERT·MEANS·HOUSE
AMHERST·NEW·HAMPSHIRE

Detail of Mantel in the Parlor
COLONEL ROBERT MEANS HOUSE, AMHERST, NEW HAMPSHIRE

Landing on Main Stairway
COLONEL ROBERT MEANS HOUSE, AMHERST, NEW HAMPSHIRE

Window on Stair Landing
COLONEL ROBERT MEANS HOUSE, AMHERST, NEW HAMPSHIRE

South Doorway

Back Staircase

COLONEL ROBERT MEANS HOUSE, AMHERST, NEW HAMPSHIRE

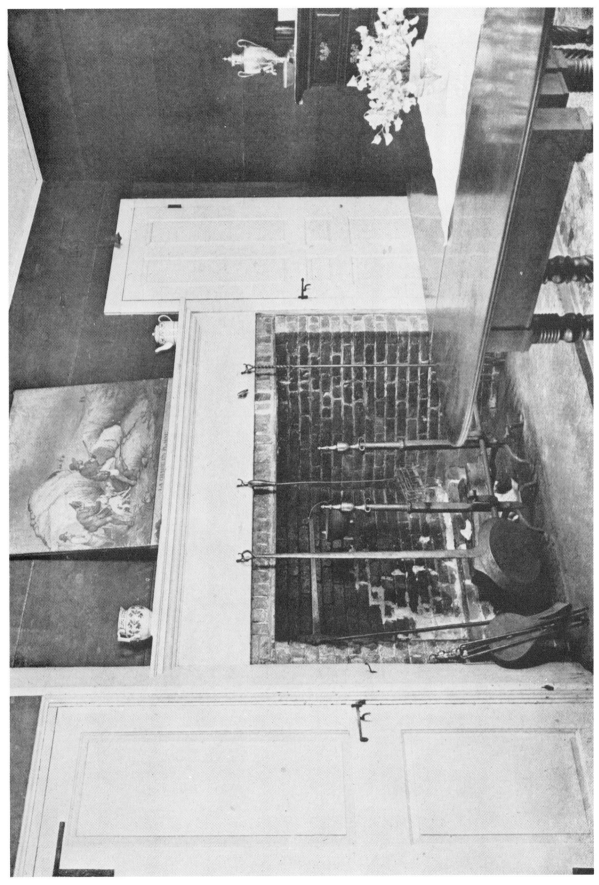

Original Kitchen, Now Used as a Dining Room
COLONEL ROBERT MEANS HOUSE, AMHERST, NEW HAMPSHIRE

Detail of Window
COLONEL ROBERT MEANS HOUSE, AMHERST, NEW HAMPSHIRE

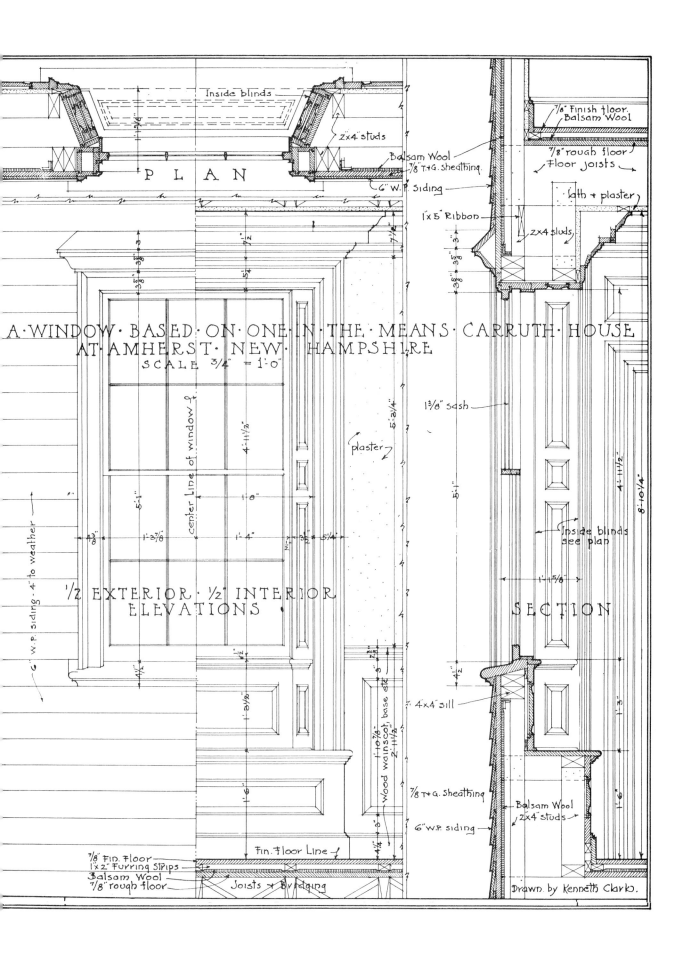

P L A N

Inside blinds

2x4 studs

Balsam Wool
⅞" T+G. sheathing
6" W.P. siding

1x5" Ribbon

⅞" Finish floor.
Balsam Wool

⅞" rough floor
Floor Joists

lath + plaster

2x4 studs

1⅜" sash

plaster

center Line of window

A·WINDOW·BASED·ON·ONE·IN·THE·MEANS·CARRUTH·HOUSE
AT·AMHERST·NEW·HAMPSHIRE
SCALE ¾" = 1'·0"

½ EXTERIOR · ½ INTERIOR
ELEVATIONS

Inside blinds
see plan

S E C T I O N

Wood wainscot, base etc

Fin. Floor Line

4x4" sill

⅞" T+G. Sheathing

6" W.P. siding

Balsam Wool
2x4 studs

⅞" Fin. Floor
1x2" Furring Strips
Balsam Wool
⅞" rough floor

Joists + Bridging

6" W.P. siding - 4" to weather

Drawn by Kenneth Clark.

Detail of Main Cornice
COLONEL ROBERT MEANS HOUSE, AMHERST, NEW HAMPSHIRE

Colonel Paul Wentworth Mansion

Text by
Frank Chouteau Brown
Photographs by
Arthur C. Haskell
Originally published in 1939 as White Pine Monograph
Volume XXV, Number 4

View From Southwest, on Original Site (1936)

COL. PAUL WENTWORTH MANSION—1701—SALMON FALLS, NEW HAMPSHIRE

THE INTERIOR DETAILS AND FURNISHINGS OF THE COL. PAUL WENTWORTH MANSION BUILT IN 1701 AT SALMON FALLS, NEW HAMPSHIRE, AND REMOVED TO DOVER, MASSACHUSETTS, IN 1937

THE Wentworth Mansion at Salmon Falls was built by a grandson of Elder William Wentworth, born in England in 1617, who came to this country in 1639 to found an American branch of an old and famous English family. Many of his descendants still reside in and about Portsmouth, New Hampshire. The dwelling built by the Elder's oldest son, Samuel, probably about 1670, just "south of Liberty Ridge and Puddle Dock," was in existence up to about 1926, and its principal room and staircase are now incorporated in the American Wing of the Metropolitan Museum, in New York City.

The fourth son of Elder William was Ezekiel (born 1651) who had six children. Ezekiel's second son (born in 1678) was Paul, and his third son was Benjamin, whose son, John, inherited the Salmon Falls property from his uncle, by a will made in 1747–1748. Paul was a first cousin of Governor Benning Wentworth (born 1696) whose father had been brought up with his on Garrison Hill, nearby, in Dover, New Hampshire. Paul's father, Ezekiel, had settled at Salmon Falls, and it was therefore easy for his son, Paul, to establish himself on the top of a commanding knoll, nearby the falls named from the salmon that came up the river. There he established a sawmill, and conducted a profitable business in supplying lumber for the rapidly growing and important town of Portsmouth, at the river's mouth, and for export to England. A more detailed description of the family inter-relationships, along with the various important Portsmouth dwellings with which they are associated, may be found in *Old Time New England*, Vol. XIX, No. 2, for October, 1928.

Long before 1936, the water power at Salmon Falls had caused the town to develop into a manufacturing community; the railroad had been carried directly in front of the old house; and it was no longer a suitable or pleasant site for the later generations of the family, who still owned the old mansion. In order to preserve the structure and continue it in use, therefore, it was taken down in the fall of 1936, piece by piece, and transported to an appropriately rural — if quite different — site, beside another river, in Dover, Massachusetts, where it could become the home of new generations. And in the process of taking the old dwelling apart, many details of its past use and history were disclosed, to the recording of which this present publication is to be principally restricted.

First it should be said that as the house stood in Salmon Falls it contained no recent or "modern" improvements. No plumbing or heating had ever been added. It had been occupied of late years only in summer, and kept practically as a residential museum; the family, when in residence, having meals in the old barn nearby, which had been equipped with more modern cooking conveniences. And the house, when removed, has been as carefully maintained in all its original rooms, with no change, other than to introduce some inconspicuous electric and heating outlets. A small, but conveniently modern, kitchen has been installed, with a maid's room over, in an eighteen foot extension of the old "Beverly Ell" to the east. The old fireplace in the "lean-to kitchen" has been restored, and the kitchen made, by inconspicuous minor changes, into the actual living room of the house. The lean-to was widened by three feet, to obtain necessary room, so that all modern plumbing, closets, etc., could be contained within the old "dark attic" in the lean-to over the kitchen, the original appearance of which is shown on page 212, while the minor rearrangements made across the rear of the first floor plan have been indicated on the top of the measured drawing on page 206. As all the paneling in the various rooms — except one — had been in-

View From Northeast, on Original Site (1935)

View From Northwest, on Original Site (1936)
COL. PAUL WENTWORTH MANSION — 1701 — SALMON FALLS, NEW HAMPSHIRE

stalled after smaller fire-places had been built within the original large openings, it was impossible to restore the original fireplaces, except in the lean-to kitchen-living room. The old fire-place originally in the dining room, was uncovered, however, and installed at Dover, Massachusetts, in the new basement room immediately below the old dining room.

The original house was built as a four-room dwelling, with the usual central chimney and staircase against its south face, with casement windows, and a double

View From Southwest, on New Site Dover, Massachusetts (1939)

width entrance doorway. Upon the rear, facing north, there were only three small, single casements and a kitchen door, which (according to the old accounts) connected through a low shed-like structure with the barn, at the northeast of the dwelling. The space along the low shed attic was the slaves quarters. The plate on page 207 shows the original appearance of this house as well as the idea of its structural skeleton frame, with some of the more important timber jointings. The same plate also shows the framing of the later

Looking across Vestibule into Pine Room at West (Dover)
COL. PAUL WENTWORTH MANSION — 1701 — SALMON FALLS, NEW HAMPSHIRE

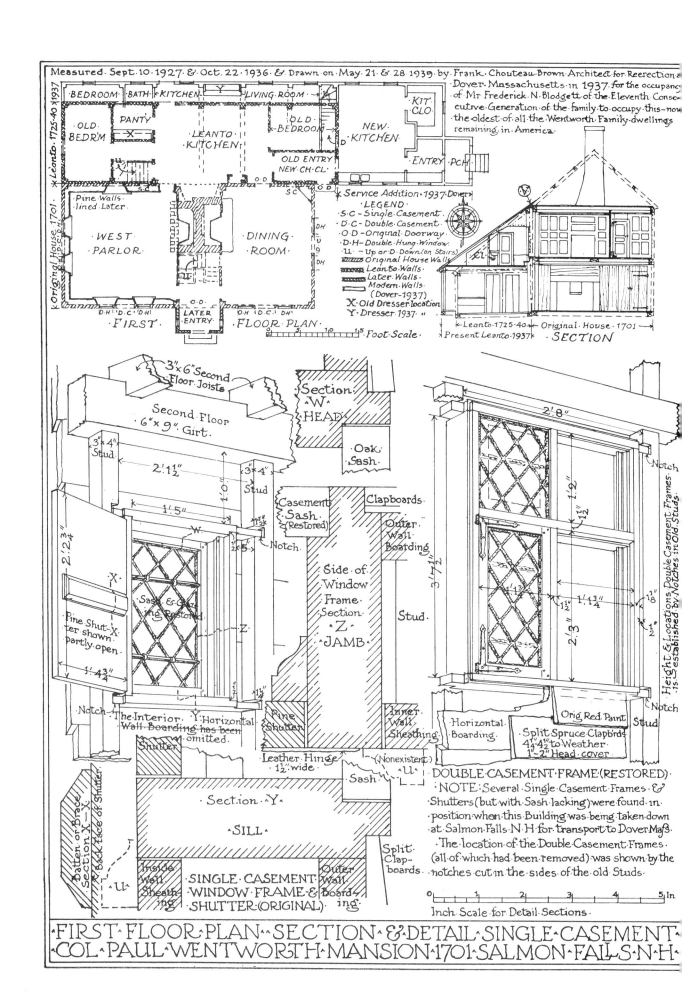

FIRST·FLOOR·PLAN··SECTION·&·DETAIL·SINGLE·CASEMENT·
COL·PAUL·WENTWORTH·MANSION·1701·SALMON·FALLS·S·N·H·

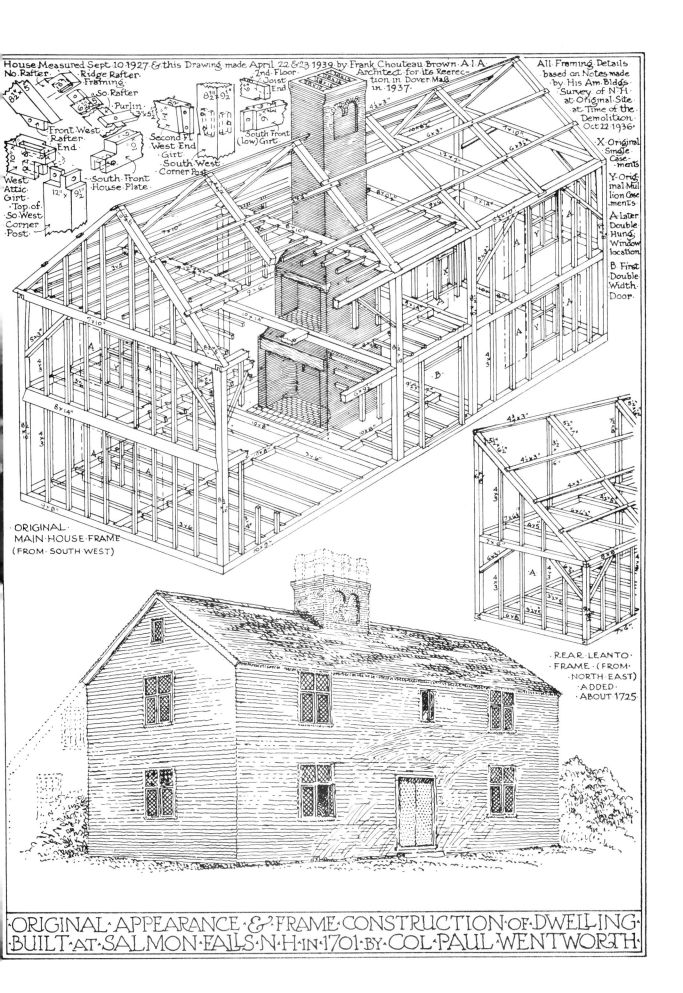

House Measured Sept 10 1927 & this Drawing made April 22 & 23 1939 by Frank Chouteau Brown A.I.A. Architect for its Reerection in Dover Mass in 1937.

No. Rafter. Ridge Rafter. Framing. 2nd Floor Joist End. So. Rafter. Purlin. Front West Rafter End. Second Fl. West End Girt. South West Corner Post. South Front (low) Girt. South Front House Plate. West Attic Girt. Top of So. West Corner Post.

All Framing Details based on Notes made by His Am. Bldgs Survey of N.H. at Original Site at Time of the Demolition Oct 22 1936.

X Original Single Casements.

Y Original Mullion Casements.

A later Double Hung Window location.

B First Double Width Door.

ORIGINAL MAIN HOUSE FRAME (FROM SOUTH WEST)

REAR LEANTO FRAME (FROM NORTH EAST) ADDED ABOUT 1725.

ORIGINAL APPEARANCE & FRAME CONSTRUCTION OF DWELLING BUILT AT SALMON FALLS N·H IN 1701 BY COL PAUL WENTWORTH

Staircase, Second Flight to Attic, Original State

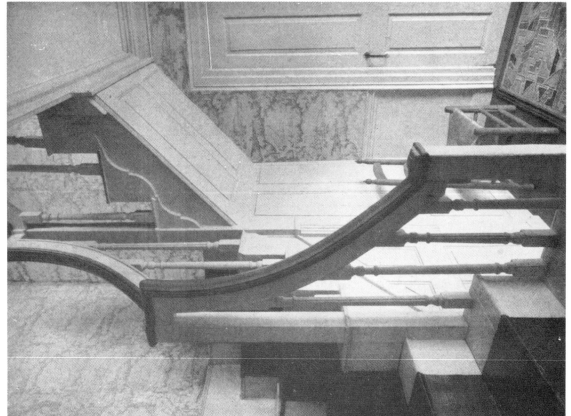

Later Staircase, First Flight From Front Vestibule

COL. PAUL WENTWORTH MANSION — 1701 — SALMON FALLS, NEW HAMPSHIRE

Original Kitchen Fireplace, as Restored at Dover

Original Living Room Fireplace, Restored at Dover

COL. PAUL WENTWORTH MANSION—1701—NOW AT DOVER, MASSACHUSETTS

General View Across Dining Room From Hall Door

Dining Room Paneled Side and Fireplace
COL. PAUL WENTWORTH MANSION—1701—SALMON FALLS, NEW HAMPSHIRE

Pine West Parlor, View From Hall Doorway

Detail of Fireplace and Wall Toward Stair Hall, West Parlor
COL. PAUL WENTWORTH MANSION — 1701 — SALMON FALLS, NEW HAMPSHIRE

lean-to, added sometime between 1725 and 1740—unusual from the fact that it had a frame completely separate from the main house, as appears distinctly in the section at the head of page 206, where a space of about seven inches at the point marked "V," between the two frames, was spanned only by the roof shingling.

While none of the double-casement frames was found in position, there could be no doubt as to their location and dimensions, as the notches into which these window frames fitted were disclosed in the original wall studding. Contrary to the usual belief, that double-hung windows were added

Old Lean-To, or "Dark Attic," Looking East

at the original window locations, which were widened and lowered for that purpose, the frame structure on page 207 and the floor plan at the top of page 206 show that the larger casements were centered in the rooms, and when the double-hung frames were added, they were placed *out*side the studs that had been set each side of the original double casements. This fact explains the somewhat closer spacing of the pairs of double-hung windows; and may be the reason for the similarly closer spacing that occurs on many another old house, as well!

An unusual contribution to our knowledge of old

Paneled Chamber, Looking Toward Original Fireplace
COL. PAUL WENTWORTH MANSION—1701—SALMON FALLS, NEW HAMPSHIRE

East Family Chamber, Looking Toward North End, Showing Old Wall Paper

East Family Chamber, Looking Toward Fireplace Side (Dover, 1939)
COL. PAUL WENTWORTH MANSION — 1701 — SALMON FALLS, NEW HAMPSHIRE

Detail of Double-Faced Partition in Pine Chamber

Detail of Northwest Corner in Pine Parlor

COL. PAUL WENTWORTH MANSION—1701—SALMON FALLS, NEW HAMPSHIRE

building customs was made by the several single casement frames, which were found in place in the walls, covered by later paneling or changes, with their interior wooden shutters, fully shown on page 206. These windows, along with some old split spruce clapboards, which still showed the old red paint, and rear eaves trim had been preserved under the lean-to.

Old Lean-to Kitchen Looking West, Salmon Falls

The one in the second story closet-room, back of the chimney, was easily seen in the attic in Salmon Falls. Unfortunately, none of these windows had retained either the sash or the leading; which have been supplied from contemporaneous material, along with the restoration of the double-casement window, developed to fit the spaces and notches found in the old house frame. The upper opening is shown with a fixed leaded filling, though a sash, if installed (as seems unlikely) has been outlined by dotted lines.

But meanwhile, the double-hung sash windows had been installed in the principal rooms, even before the lean-to was added, as clearly appeared in the arrangement of the pine paneling on the north walls of the two rooms west of the fireplace. The pine walls in the west parlor were probably added at this same time; but the double-faced partition and paneling in the bedroom over—despite the fact that this is the only room preserving the original fireplace—was probably added at a still later date; as was also the vestibule built

out at the front entrance, and the changed staircase of the first flight, with its pine balustered rail. The original rail and buttress were left in the runs from the second to the attic floor.

The paneling in the two east rooms was also of later date, and the corner cupboard (which will later be shown more fully in detail) was the result of at least two further changes. The very early wall paper in the east second story bedroom, still displaying the tax stamp with the English crown, was moved (along with the section of plaster wall upon which it was pasted), in one panel, the only piece of original plaster preserved in the dwelling in its new location.

The lean-to kitchen (shown above, as it last stood at Salmon Falls) was the only old room much altered by the necessary uses of the various intervening generations. Its old windows had full-length sliding shutters, and beneath its floor was a shallow circular pit—or "Indian cellar"—with original movable steps from the trap-door in the floor above. The original kitchen fireplace has been rebuilt in Dover, with the old bricks, and the one from the west parlor is restored in a room with primitive furniture and fittings, (page 209) beneath the present dining room. The original kitchen dresser (to be illustrated in a later chapter) was found in the pantry and replaced in the kitchen-living room, between two windows at north wall.

View From River Bank (From Northwest)
New Kitchen End and Garage at Left
PAUL WENTWORTH MANSION, DOVER

Old Lean-to Kitchen With Original Fireplace (Restored) Looking Southwest
COL. PAUL WENTWORTH MANSION—1701—NOW AT DOVER, MASSACHUSETTS

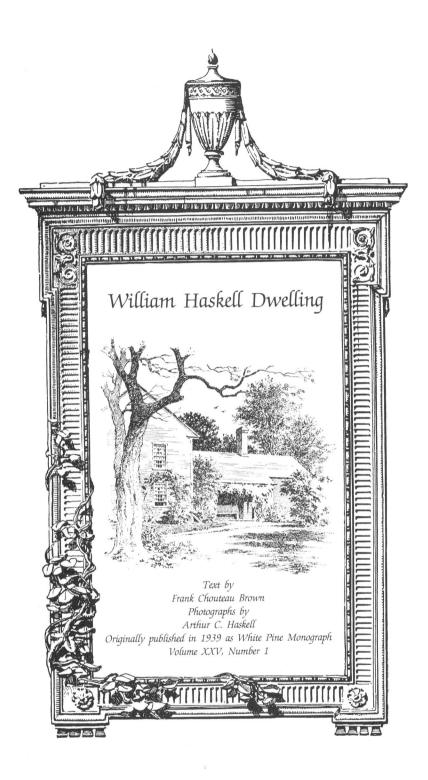

William Haskell Dwelling

Text by
Frank Chouteau Brown
Photographs by
Arthur C. Haskell
Originally published in 1939 as White Pine Monograph
Volume XXV, Number 1

Fireplace Detail, First Floor Living Room
WILLIAM HASKELL DWELLING, WEST GLOUCESTER, MASSACHUSETTS

THE INTERIOR DETAILS AND FURNISHINGS OF THE WILLIAM HASKELL DWELLING BUILT BEFORE 1650 AT WEST GLOUCESTER, MASSACHUSETTS

SOMETHING has already been told in this series (Volume X, Chapter 8 and Volume VII, Chapter 2) of the early history of the Cape Ann settlements, although not in detail. It remains a varied and confusing record. However, after three years, the first settlement of 1623 was given up. This was the Dorchester Company, whose members returned to England, except the few who followed Roger Conant to Naumkeag, and became the "Old Planters" of Salem history. Besides the temporary fish drying stages set up by the men from Plymouth, in 1624, and the brief stop of the *Talbot*, en route to Salem in June of 1630, there is also the legend that the region harbored for a while the gay Thomas Morton, after his expulsion from Merrymount, near Quincy, by the more sober-minded Pilgrims.

At least two other attempts at settlement were made, in 1633, by a group under Rev. John Robinson, of Plymouth; and another "Fishing Colony," authorized in 1639, to one "Maurice Thomson, merchant." Neither succeeded; but it would appear that the region was gradually becoming populated because, in 1641, the General Court appointed a committee to "view and settle bounds" of Ipswich, Cape Ann and Jeffries Creek (later to become Manchester). This was done in February of the following year, 1642, only the year before William Haskell removed from Beverly to "Planter's Neck."

It was in 1637 that there came to the new world from Bristol, England, three brothers, all of whom at first established themselves within the area of the old Salem Colony. The eldest, Roger, born in 1613, remained in Salem until his death in 1667. The second brother, William, who was born in 1617 and died in 1693; shortly after his arrival in Beverly removed to Cape Ann. The third and youngest, Mark, born in 1620, settled and lived in Beverly, which was then a part of Salem.

William Haskell removed from Beverly to "Glos-ter," in 1643, when he was about 26 years old, and was married to Mary, daughter of Walter Tybbots of that colony, on November 16 of that same year. In 1645 his name is mentioned as owner of property on "Planter's Neck," a promontory lying between Lobster Cove and the ocean, on the northerly side of Cape Ann, in "Agassquam," now known as Annisquam. There he resided until either 1652, or shortly thereafter (some family histories say 1656). At any rate, on August 4, 1652 there is a record of the transfer of about ten acres, with a house and barn, from Richard Window, to Deacon William Haskell, on the west side of Walker's Creek, and the Annisquam River, in what is now known as West Gloucester.

Sometime during this early period, there appeared on the passenger list of a small vessel sailing to this colony, one Richard Window, who was there described as a "joyner." He located upon the west, or mainland, side of the Annisquam River, which even then nearly separated the Cape from the mainland. This appears to have been the same property that was later transferred, with house and barns, to Deacon Haskell in 1652. Exactly when Window built his house has not been determined, although two dates mentioned are 1645 and 1648. Even if Deacon Haskell built a new house after acquiring this property in 1652, its antiquity remains sufficiently established, and as much might still be said, if it was even built for the occupancy of his eldest son, William, after his marriage in 1667! Based upon any one of these dates, the preservation of this essential fabric, in so comparatively unchanged an estate, over all the years between, is one of those happy miracles that have occurred in only a few of our early New England structures.

The only argument against the house having been built at the earliest dates given—1645 or 1648—is that its structure proves that it was all constructed at one time, and a "two room" two-story house, in that remote location, at so early a date, seems rather pretentious, when comparing it with the small "one room" Riggs Cottage, across the river, for instance, which was built within a few years of 1658, one of the several hewn log houses on the Cape (and undoubtedly built with*out* benefit of instructions from the Delaware Swedes!). Yet Richard Window, as the "joiner" for the colony, might well have chosen to express his skill in his own dwelling, even at so early a date and in the comparative isolation of its site.

The original structure—still easily to be distinguished from the two principal additions that now adjoin its outer walls—had the usual early plan, of two rooms upon each floor, each side of a large central chimney, with the staircase to the upper story built against the chimney front. The house faces south, and is but thirty-six feet front by eighteen feet deep. Each story is about 7' 5" high, from the floor to the under side of the single thickness of boarding forming the floor above. The later plaster ceilings fortunately preserved the old vermilion color that had been used at some earlier time to pick out the slightly-moulded lower edge of the beams over the larger room a treatment that has been repeated up and down the chamfered edges of the heavy oak corner posts in this same room.

In summer time, despite its location near a main highway, the house is so protected by the trees along the brook, that it is approached in apparent isolation over a narrow dirt roadway that at first discloses only its old front, unaltered since the old casement sash were exchanged for double-hung windows early in the eighteenth century, and the roof and outer wall faces, which have required occasional renewal from time to time.

The present entrance door is a replacement. Within its simple framework, with old boards and still older bosses, the door itself, hung on old wrought iron angled strap hinges, and graced with a wooden bolt upon its inner face, is one of the several successful additions made by the present owners, Mr. A. H. Atkins, a well known sculptor, and his wife. Shortly after acquiring the house, Mr. Atkins was so fortunate as to find an old box containing enough old hand-made

iron bosses (which had apparently never been used) to complete the illusion of authentic antiquity for this entrance that the house deserves.

To avoid making any changes in the old structure, Mr. Atkins moved up against the back of the dwelling, upon one end, an old shed upon the estate, and made its interior over into a bedroom, building a new chimney at its northern end, in which he copied one of the old fireplaces from the front house. There was also a simple shed-like structure extending eastward from the rear portion of that end of the dwelling, containing a minute kitchen that, with the entry in the lean-to, provided a small dining space and lavatory off the guest room. Within the last few years (indeed, since the major number of these pictures were taken) this end has been replaced with a somewhat larger wing containing a dining room, as well as a kitchen, and in the second story, another bedroom and a couple of small baths to serve that room, as well as the old east bedroom, from which it is unobtrusively entered, from an old closet space between. By these means, the owners secured for themselves all needed modern conveniences, and a larger capacity for the dwelling, without in any way injuring its exterior appearance, or disturbing the restful interior character of its older nucleus.

Entering, as most people do, through the door opening from the old stable yard into the lean-to along the back of the dwelling, the early note is struck immediately by the few simple early chairs and table set along this miniature gallery, and the fine collection of pewter shown upon the open shelves of the small cupboard against the rear wall of the old house. This entry is plastered after the old fashion, exposing the hand-worked wooden principal timbers in the ceiling and at the corners of the space enclosed.

From this room you step down—over the old raised sill of the original house—into the larger, or living, room of the dwelling; although it contains the smaller fireplace, as the other first story room, to the west, was the old kitchen or hall, with its wider, deeper and higher fireplace, containing an inner corner baking oven and warming niche. But the east room is

·FIRST·FLOOR·PLAN·
·WILLIAM·HASKELL·DWELLING·WEST·GLOUCESTER·MAS·

Front Elevation From the Southeast

Rear Elevation From Northeast
WILLIAM HASKELL DWELLING, WEST GLOUCESTER, MASSACHUSETTS

*Second Story Passage Looking Toward
Spinning Room*

for two stories, from sill to plate, relieved only by shallow "shadow moulding" along the exposed inner edges. The difficulties of obtaining plaster from old Indian shell heaps caused chimneys and fireplaces to be laid in puddled clay, as was here done, and the few finer natural lime deposits—when found—were reserved for lime washes or plaster wall bases. It was rarely wasted on room ceilings.

This completes the original dwelling, but still gives no suggestion of the beautiful and completely appropriate outfitting that the old place has so sympathetically received from its present owners. For that suggestion one must turn to the accompanying pictures, in which have been recorded a small portion of the many compositions that exist to delight the eye, in whatever direction one turns, anywhere within the structure. For not only are its occupants appreciative of the dwelling, but they are also appreciative—and have been acquisitive, as well!—of all the early types of furnishings for which it supplies such unique and appropriate backgrounds.

In one room after the other, one finds old housekeeping equipment of the period—and of the several generations of the old family that followed (for four generations, at least, the "eldest son of the eldest son" was a William Haskell). The rooms are crowded

a very little more pretentious—if indeed, the word can be used at all in reference to so simple an entity as this Haskell dwelling—with its delicately edge-moulded hewn oak beams, the shaped and chamfered cornerposts, and the simple toothed moulding over the fire opening, and below the inclined featheredged paneled boarding that extends from the old fire-lintel to the chimney girt above.

In the front entry, more spacious than usual for so small a plan, the plainest possible flight of steep stairs rises back of the single thickness of featheredged boarding, exposed on both faces. Between this and the uncovered brick face of the chimney, the flight rises from winders at the start, to a narrow space before the door of the west chamber, probably the spinning room, just wide enough to allow a person to turn and pass across to the large east chamber, at the other end of the main house.

As in most early structures, the building was probably left entirely unfinished inside its framed and boarded walls. The simple boarding separating the front stairs from the entry, and finishing the fireplace room ends, was then entirely consistent with the exterior walls. In other examples of this period, the outer wall boarding sometimes extended continuously

Entry, First Floor, Looking into Old Kitchen

Living Room Showing Door to Rear Lean-to

Living Room Looking Toward Front Entrance

WILLIAM HASKELL DWELLING, WEST GLOUCESTER, MASSACHUSETTS

Old Kitchen, Looking Northeast

WILLIAM HASKELL DWELLING, WEST GLOUCESTER, MASSACHUSETTS

Old Kitchen, Wall Opposite Fireplace

Old Kitchen, Showing Door to Front Entry
WILLIAM HASKELL DWELLING,
WEST GLOUCESTER, MASSACHUSETTS

with early impedimenta; old iron and wooden fittings, cranes, trammels and trammel hooks; iron trivets, skillets, pots, kettles, candlesticks, and dogs; foot stools, shovels, tongs, and coal pinchers; wooden trenchers, pewter porringers, plates and bowls. Early glazed slipware, or pewter and wooden mixing bowls, are near at hand, with early oak, hickory and maple or pine chairs; tables, benches and stools set handily beside the fireplace or across the room. Even wall rack pipe holders, pine knife boxes, etc., are there.

The pieces of early glass are less conspicuous, but

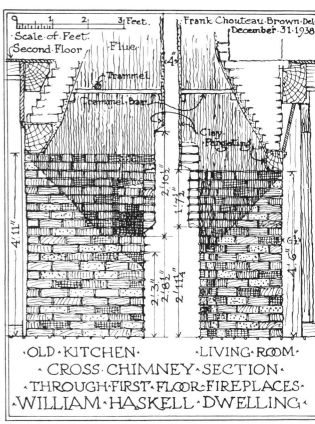

·OLD·KITCHEN·   ·LIVING·ROOM·
· CROSS·CHIMNEY·SECTION·
·THROUGH·FIRST·FLOOR·FIREPLACES·
·WILLIAM·HASKELL·DWELLING·

they, too, are grouped thereabouts, as needed, along with appropriate textiles, simple hooked rugs, slight small print sash curtains, and woven bedcovers. Even the guest chamber in the attached shed-ell, is fitted as finely and beautifully as the more authentic rooms. In fact, the whole structure and its contents, as it stands, composes as complete and perfect a "museum" of early *Americana* as now remains in New England representative of its date and time. In proof thereof we tender for the reader's delectation some few of the many glimpses of these interiors and their furnishings, such as the painstaking craft and skill of a descendant of the younger brother of the first William Haskell now makes possible!

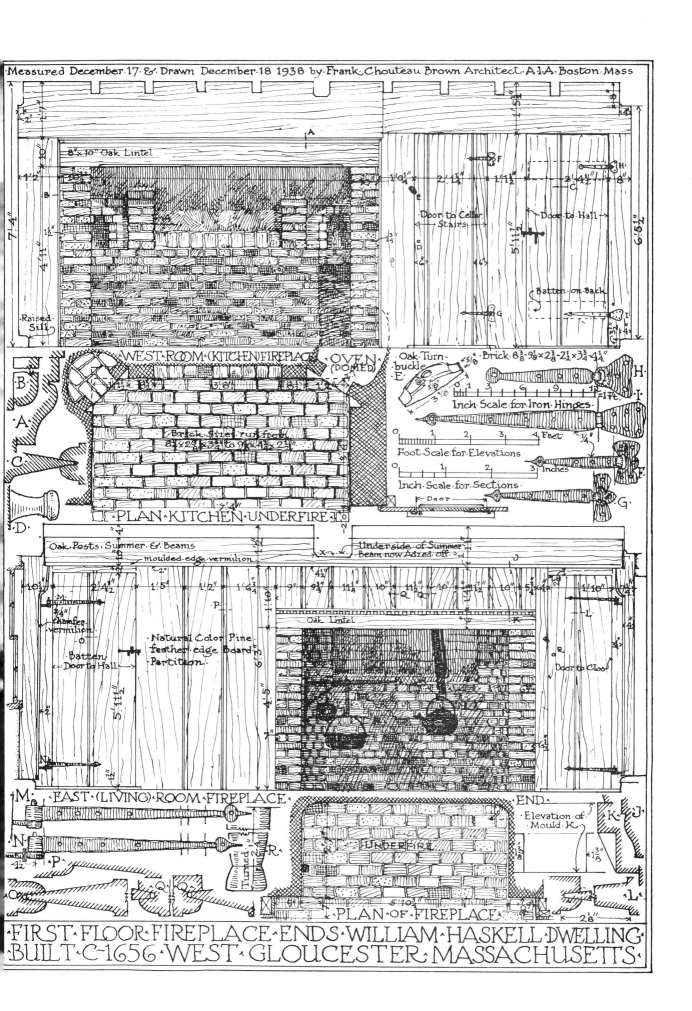

Measured December 17 & Drawn December 18 1938 by Frank Chouteau Brown Architect A.I.A. Boston Mass

8"x10" Oak Lintel

Raised Sill

Door to Cellar Stairs

Door to Hall

Batten on Back

WEST ROOM (KITCHEN) FIREPLACE · OVEN (DOMED)

Oak Turn-buckle E.

Brick 8⅜–9⅛ × 2¾–2½ × 3¾–4⅛

Inch Scale for Iron Hinges

Foot Scale for Elevations

Inch Scale for Sections

Door

PLAN KITCHEN UNDERFIRE

Brick Size Run from 8¼ × 2¼ & 3¾ to 9⅛ × 4¼ × 2½"

Oak Posts, Summer & Beams
moulded edge vermilion

Underside of Summer Beam now Adzed off

Natural Color Pine feather edge Boards Partition

Oak Lintel

¾" Chamfer. vermilion

Batten Door to Hall

Door to Closet

EAST (LIVING) ROOM FIREPLACE

END.
Elevation of Mould K

Turned 2¼"

UNDERFIRE

PLAN OF FIREPLACE

FIRST·FLOOR·FIREPLACE·ENDS·WILLIAM·HASKELL·DWELLING·
BUILT·C·1656·WEST·GLOUCESTER·MASSACHUSETTS·

Living Room, General View Looking Toward Northeast
WILLIAM HASKELL DWELLING, WEST GLOUCESTER, MASSACHUSETTS

Old Kitchen, Showing Door to Guest Room Ell
WILLIAM HASKELL DWELLING, WEST GLOUCESTER, MASSACHUSETTS

Guest Room, South End with Door to Old Kitchen

Lean-to Gallery Looking Toward East End
WILLIAM HASKELL DWELLING, WEST GLOUCESTER, MASSACHUSETTS

Bedroom over Old Kitchen, Looking Northwest

Bedroom over Living Room, Looking Northwest
WILLIAM HASKELL DWELLING, WEST GLOUCESTER, MASSACHUSETTS

Spinning Room Chamber, Southwest Corner
WILLIAM HASKELL DWELLING, WEST GLOUCESTER, MASSACHUSETTS

Gardner-White-Pingree House

Text by
Frank Chouteau Brown
Photographs by
Arthur C. Haskell
Originally published in 1940 as White Pine Monograph
Volume XXVI, Number 4

Entrance Hall and Stairway
GARDNER-WHITE-PINGREE HOUSE—1804—SALEM, MASSACHUSETTS
Samuel McIntire, Architect

THE GARDNER-WHITE-PINGREE HOUSE
BUILT IN SALEM, MASSACHUSETTS, IN 1804
BY SAMUEL McINTIRE, ARCHITECT

AMONG the artisans of New England the name and fame of Samuel McIntire has spread far beyond the local boundaries of his native town of Salem, Massachusetts. Although probably best known as a carver of wood, he is also to be credited with the actual design of many of the mansions in and about Salem, with which his name is still associated — and while his abilities as a designer were not — in his early years — commensurate with his skill as a woodworker, among his later structures may be found examples of a refinement and perfection in treatment that are not to be bettered by any among his contemporaries.

His father, Joseph McIntire, was also a "housewright," or carpenter — as we would term him today. Samuel was born January 16, 1757, and had two brothers, both of whom were also trained in his father's shop, and later assisted Samuel to complete many of the houses of local McIntire fame — thus considerably extending the period of years and number of houses with which the name could be associated!

His elder brother, Joseph, later became his principal assistant. He was born nine years before Samuel, and still another assistant — his younger brother by two years — was Angier. Samuel McIntire had also a son, Samuel F. McIntire, who assisted his father; as was also true of the sons of his elder brother, Joseph. So, actually, we have the name of McIntire associated with the buildings of Salem for a period of three generations, or probably about seventy-five years, including the working years of his father! Samuel himself died in 1811, but left behind him many drawings and designs, as well as the large school of relatives and assistants who had been helping him.

Early in life he bought a house at 31 Summer Street, Salem, in which he lived, and built his shop in the rear of the dwelling. This house was built in 1780, and as Samuel McIntire's best known early house is the Pierce-Johannot-Nichols Mansion, which was started in 1782, he must from the first have been very successful in business. Despite the delicacy of his carvings and their design, his early buildings were over-bold and of heavy relief — of which this house provides an excellent example. Later, his style of design became more refined, but remained somewhat ornate and still "heavy" in character — as in the Cook-Oliver dwelling, perhaps — and it was not until his later years, that he acquired the experience and feeling that made possible the simplicity and distinction that is to be found in the David Pingree House, the example chosen for detailed illustration here.

This dwelling — lately known as the Gardner-White-Pingree House, and numbered 128 Essex Street — fortunately has been preserved through its acquisition by the Essex Institute, and is representative of McIntire's third and best period. The sheer simplicity of this house façade is characteristic — the relation of story above story, with only a slightly-projecting band of marble to mark the floor lines between; the windows set almost flush with the wall face, and no other ornament except the flush marble lintels and the charmingly naïve porch, up to the cornice and eaves balustrade above! But lack of pretentious detail is compensated by its perfect scale and the proportion of all its parts. Those who desire more elaboration may turn to the interior, where equal restraint, along with great delicacy of carving, ornaments the mantels, staircase, door frames, and cornices throughout.

The interiors have been very carefully furnished from the collections of the Essex Institute, and individuals interested, including Mr. William Endicott, and others. As a result, some rooms are simple and dignified, while others are definitely more gay and provocative, especially in their color schemes and draperies.

The dining room conforms to the first classification, with simple blue-toned wall, and Venetian blinds. The two rooms on the eastern side are more frivolous. The front room windows have simple draped underpieces of plain gauze or muslin, with parti-colored fringe, re-echoing the sprigs of embroidered, flowering sprays on the draped muslin overpiece. The rear room has a similar window material, all in white, with white embroidered sprays. In both rooms the walls are covered with strong yellow paper, plain in the front room, and with panels of classical subjects breaking up the width in the rear parlor. In both, a classical frieze goes above the dado, and a nar-

Upper Part Entrance Porch Detail

row band below the cornice, with a vine edging the wall openings—all printed in shades of blue.

The second floor front room draperies are peachblow silk, with a peach and blue-striped similar material festooned above the hangings. A similar arrangement of this material forms the posted bed canopy. The bedroom at the rear has blue watered silk at the windows and pale tinted walls. The larger west room has a light blue tinted plaster wall, with an East Indian damask with rosebuds, blue cords and tassels at the windows, and the bed is covered with blue brocade.

Front Façade and Entrance Porch
GARDNER-WHITE-PINGREE HOUSE—1804—SALEM, MASSACHUSETTS
Samuel McIntire, Architect

Detail of Mantel in Front Drawing Room
GARDNER-WHITE-PINGREE HOUSE—1804—SALEM, MASSACHUSETTS
Samuel McIntire, Architect

Detail Showing Turn of Stair Rail to Second Floor

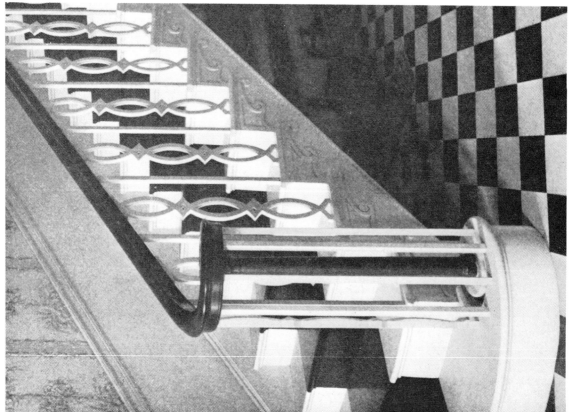

Detail of Newel and Start of Stairs

GARDNER-WHITE-PINGREE HOUSE — 1804 — SALEM, MASSACHUSETTS

Samuel McIntire, Architect

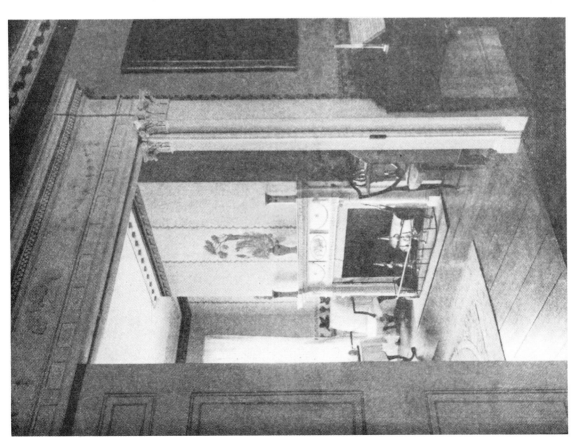

Corner of Hall Inside Entrance Doorway

GARDNER-WHITE-PINGREE HOUSE — 1804 — SALEM, MASSACHUSETTS

Samuel McIntire, Architect

View into North Parlor from Front Drawing Room

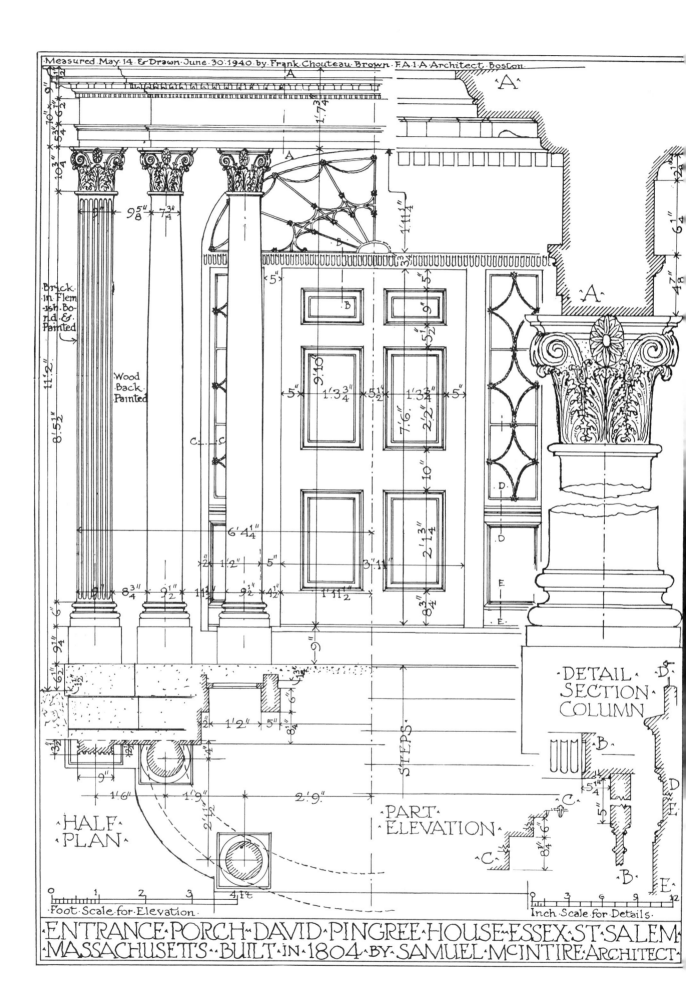

Measured May 14 & Drawn June 30 1940 by Frank Chouteau Brown F.A.I.A. Architect Boston

'A'

Brick in Flemish Bond & Painted

Wood Back Painted

'A'

DETAIL SECTION COLUMN

HALF PLAN

PART ELEVATION

STEPS

0   1   2   3   4 Ft
Foot Scale for Elevation

0   3   6   9   12
Inch Scale for Details

ENTRANCE·PORCH·DAVID·PINGREE·HOUSE·ESSEX·ST·SALEM
MASSACHUSETTS·BUILT·IN·1804·BY·SAMUEL·MCINTIRE·ARCHITECT

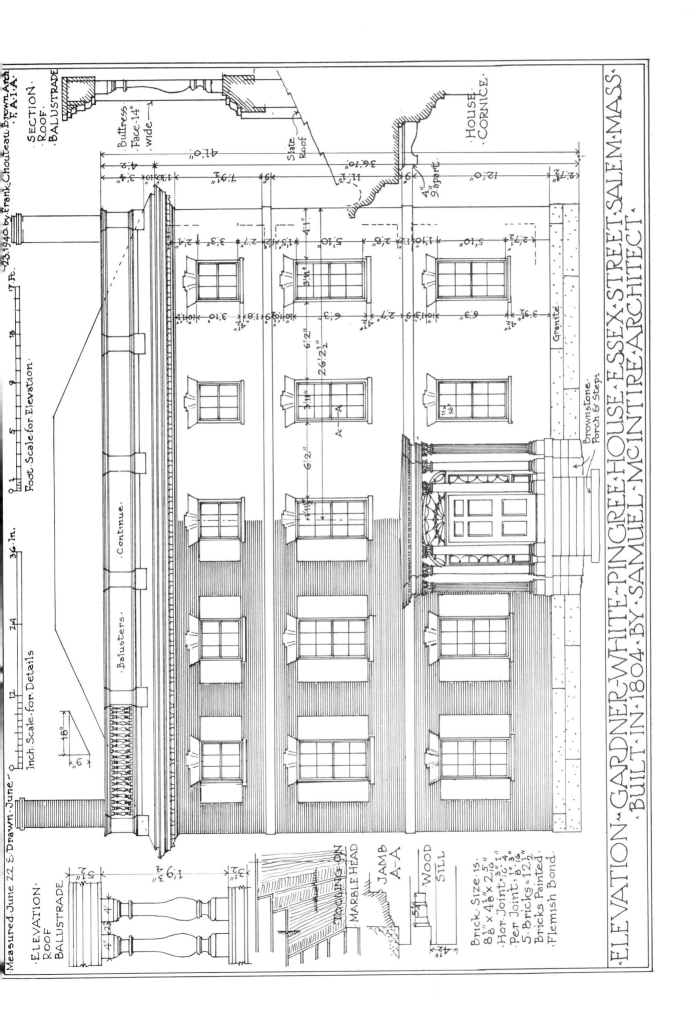

Measured June 22 · E · Drawn June ~ -23 · 1940 · by · Frank · Chouteau · Brown · Arch · F · A · I · A ·

SECTION.
ROOF.
BALUSTRADE

Buttress Face 14" wide

Slate Roof

HOUSE CORNICE.

ELEVATION.
ROOF
BALUSTRADE

Foot · Scale · for · Elevation.

Inch · Scale · for · Details

18"

6"

· Balusters · · Continue ·

Granite

Brownstone Porch & Steps

BOOKING-ON
MARBLE HEAD

JAMB A–A

WOOD SILL

Brick · Size · is ·
8⅛" × 4⅛" × 2⁵⁄₁₆"
· Hor · Joint = 3¼"
· Per · Joint = ⅜ · to ⅛
5 · Bricks = 12¼"
· Bricks · Painted ·
Flemish Bond.

·ELEVATION ~ GARDNER · WHITE · PINGREE · HOUSE · ESSEX · STREET · SALEM · MASS·
·BUILT · IN · 1804 · BY · SAMUEL · MCINTIRE · ARCHITECT·

General View of Dining Room, First Floor

GARDNER-WHITE-PINGREE HOUSE — 1804 — SALEM, MASSACHUSETTS

Samuel McIntire, Architect

Front Drawing Room and Doorway to North Parlor, First Floor
GARDNER-WHITE-PINGREE HOUSE—1804—SALEM, MASSACHUSETTS
Samuel McIntire, Architect

Detail View of East Fireplace Wall, North Parlor, First Floor

GARDNER-WHITE-PINGREE HOUSE — 1804 — SALEM, MASSACHUSETTS

Samuel McIntire, Architect

Southwest Bedroom, Second Floor
GARDNER-WHITE-PINGREE HOUSE — 1804 — SALEM, MASSACHUSETTS
Samuel McIntire, Architect

Corner in North Parlor, First Floor

Corner in Front Drawing Room, First Floor

GARDNER-WHITE-PINGREE HOUSE — 1804 — SALEM, MASSACHUSETTS

Samuel McIntire, Architect

Fireplace in Northeast Bedroom, Second Floor

Corner in Southeast Bedroom, Third Floor

GARDNER-WHITE-PINGREE HOUSE — 1804 — SALEM, MASSACHUSETTS

Samuel McIntire, Architect

East Fireplace Wall of Northeast Bedroom, Second Floor

East Wall of Southeast Bedroom, Third Floor
GARDNER-WHITE-PINGREE HOUSE — 1804 — SALEM, MASSACHUSETTS
Samuel McIntire, Architect